PRAISE FOR
Baby Boomer Retirement

"Astute and provocative."
> — RICHARD KAHLENBERG, "Earthwatch Column"
> *LOS ANGELES TIMES*

"This clever guidebook will optimize the likelihood of a successful future. I've learned it's one thing to grow a home-based business into a successful public company, and an entirely different matter to parlay its rewards into a stable future."
> — FELICE WILLAT, Founder, Day Runner, Inc.
> (and a baby boomer)

"*Baby Boomer Retirement* gives the ins and outs of financial planning—an extremely informative, valuable resource. It's an important reference book to read before consulting a professional money manager. This book will help you ask all of the right questions. Whether it's kids, college, aging parents or retirement—Don Silver has given you the tools to protect your future today! I recommend that every young professional read this book."
> — LILLIAN VERNON, Chief Executive Officer
> Lillian Vernon Corporation

"I found *Baby Boomer Retirement* very valuable. It is very well written with enough of a light touch."
> — DAVID H. SOLOMON, M.D., Professor Emeritus of
> Medicine/Geriatrics and Director of the UCLA Center
> On Aging

more...

"This book has invaluable planning steps that can have a tremendous impact on a baby boomer's—or anyone's—future."
— MICHAEL GILFIX, Esq.
Co-author of *Tax, Estate & Financial Planning for the Elderly*; Fellow of the National Academy of Elder Law Attorneys; principal author of *Medi-Cal and Asset Preservation*; executive editor of *The Gilfix Elder Law Newsalert*; and member of the Advisory Board of the Stanford University Center for Biomedical Ethics

"The '65 Simple Ways to Protect Your Future' provide clear, concise, pragmatic answers! What a fantastic reference tool for the professional and the layman."
— KEVIN CONLEY, Connecticut Mutual Life Brokerage Services, Regional Brokerage Manager specializing in estate, financial and business planning (and a baby boomer)

"An easy-to-read guided tour on how to avoid the financial hazards confronting anyone concerned about their financial future. Now my clients can reach for a reliable source in this timely collection of personal financial topics."
— MARILYN ZIEMANN, CPA, in financial planning practice for 24 years (and a baby boomer)

"A very important book that's right on target!"
— SANFORD C. SIGOLOFF, President and Chairman, Sigoloff & Associates

"Excellent primer that includes all the key steps for a successful retirement."
— PHYLLIS BILLINGS, CLU, Chartered Financial Consultant

more...

"*Baby Boomer Retirement* is a simple and direct road map to a secure future."
> — ZEV YAROSLAVSKY, Councilmember, City of Los Angeles, Chairman of the Budget and Finance Committee

"It was exciting to finally read a book dedicated to helping us 'boomers' plan for our retirement years—and help our parents, too. The points and suggestions were easy to understand and follow."
> — MICHAEL J. SIEGEL, Attorney at Law (and a baby boomer)

"Clear and easy to read, this is a book to keep close at hand for reference if you have a family—spouse, children, parents —and if you want to retire comfortably."
> — PATRICK RYAN, father of a baby boomer

"Reading this book was like having our financial advisor, accountant and attorney all available at one time providing a wealth of information and advice on all the essentials of planning for retirement. It answered all the questions I had about planning for retirement and our child's educational goals but have always been too busy to take the time to learn on my own. It was easy to understand and packed with invaluable information. It allowed my husband and myself to reevaluate our situation and make better decisions about our investments and financial retirement goals."
> — LINDA HOFFMAN, Publisher, Goodman Lauren Publishing (and a baby boomer)

"Even before I finished 10 pages I started making effective use of the book."
> — STAN HOFFMAN, Urban Economist

more...

Also by Don Silver

A Parent's Guide to Wills & Trusts
(For Grandparents, Too)

BABY Boomer Retirement

65 Simple Ways to Protect Your Future

Don Silver

Adams-Hall Publishing
Los Angeles

Requests for such permissions should be addressed to:

    Adams-Hall Publishing, PO Box 491002
    Los Angeles, CA 90049-1002

No patent liability is assumed with respect to the use of the information contained herein. While every precaution has been taken in the preparation of this book, the publisher and the author assume no responsibility for errors or omissions. Neither is any liability assumed for damages resulting from the use of the information contained herein.

Library of Congress Cataloging-in-Publication Data

Silver, Don
Baby Boomer Retirement: 65 Simple Ways to Protect Your Future
      p.   cm.
    Includes index.
    ISBN 0-944708-65-X
1. Retirement income—United States—Planning. 2. Retirees—United States—Finance, Personal. 3. Baby boom generation—United States. I. Title.
HG179.S474 1994
332.024'01—dc 20   94-19422
        CIP

Cover Design by Hespenheide Design (805/373-7336)
Back cover photograph: Neil Ricklen (818/980-4969)

Adams-Hall books are available at special, quantity discounts for bulk purchases for sales promotions, premiums, fund-raising or educational use. For details, contact: Special Sales Director, Adams-Hall Publishing, PO Box 491002, Los Angeles, CA 90049-1002 (1/800-888-4452 or 310/826-1851).

Printed in the United States of America
10 9 8 7 6 5 4 3 2 1
First printing 1994   Printed on recycled paper

To Emily, Charles, Marilyn and Ralph

and especially to

Susan and Charlie

Acknowledgments

Although writing a book is a very personal process, every author needs the perspective and help of others to produce the best result.

I want to first express my thanks to those individuals who took time out of their very busy schedules to review the advance proof and offer praiseworthy comments. My deepest appreciation goes to Phyllis Billings, Judy Blythe, Kevin Conley, Marvin S. Freedman, Michael Gilfix, Linda Hoffman, Stan Hoffman, Patrick Ryan, Michael J. Siegel, Sanford C. Sigoloff, Dr. David H. Solomon, Leon C. Sterling, Lillian Vernon, Kim Villeneuve, Tim Villeneuve, Felice Willat, Zev Yaroslavsky, and Marilyn Ziemann.

Special thanks go to Phyllis Billings, Robin Hoehler, Linda Hoffman, Ralph F. Marks, Sanford C. Sigoloff, Michael J. Siegel, and Marilyn Ziemann for their helpful editorial suggestions and comments.

Gary Hespenheide of Hespenheide Design has done another wonderful cover and it has been a pleasure to work with him.

Writing a book often entails sacrifice on the part of the author balanced by support from the author's family. A special thank you to Emily, Marilyn, and Ralph for their loving support. To my young son, Charlie, let me say that Daddy looks forward to spending even more time with you now that the book is completed. Finally, I have been blessed with a loving and caring wife, Susan, who is also my best friend. I could not have written this book without her support.

Don Silver

Disclaimer

All of the names and situations in this book are hypothetical and the resemblance to anyone's actual situation is purely coincidental.

This book is intended to provide accurate information. It is not intended, however, to render any legal, tax, accounting, financial, or other professional advice or services. You should therefore use this book as a general guide only. In addition, this book contains information that was available only up to the time of printing.

Although there are certain steps described in this book that you can take yourself, this book is not intended to be a substitute for the professional assistance of an attorney, accounttant, financial planner, and life insurance agent.

Laws do change with some frequency. That's why you must discuss your situation with qualified professionals before relying solely on the information you may find here or anywhere else.

Contents

Contents

NURSING HOME NEWS

LOOKING OUT FOR YOUR PARENTS

INSURING YOUR RETIREMENT

TAKING CARE OF BUSINESS

MAKING MONEY FROM YOUR PAPERWORK

DEALING WITH INCAPACITY

Introduction

Retirement planning for baby boomers is unique and particularly challenging.

At no other time in history has a group had to confront and plan for a retirement that might last as long as 30 or 40 years. Baby boomers (those of us born between 1946 and 1964) should feel fortunate. At the turn of the century, the average American could look forward to a life span of just 47 years.

On the other hand, this longevity may force many baby boomers to continue working during "retirement," especially if the retirement years include the challenge of paying for the college education of a child or children and supporting aging parents.

A new way of thinking is needed

Perhaps the greatest challenge to us boomers is changing our thinking as a "generation of spenders" to a "generation of savers." Although we may be the best educated generation in history, our education has not prepared us to deal with pain, including the pain of being forced to save for the future. Many of us have grown up with the expectation that some person, or the government, will always be there to take care of us if necessary.

Just as we have seen how savings and loan institutions could fall apart, the same may happen to Social Security. A bipartisan panel in Congress recently warned that Social Security benefits may not be there just when baby boomers will be ready to draw on them.

Up to now, there have been three pillars of retirement planning. One of them, Social Security, needs an overhaul to be viable. The second pillar, company pension plan benefits, is being reduced or eliminated as part of the corporate down-sizing and cost-cutting trend.

What's left is the third pillar of retirement planning—personal savings and investments. In the past, personal savings and investments were seen as a way of merely enhancing an already secure retirement. For baby boomers they may be the most important component of our retirement planning. Time is on the side of baby boomers, but not for long. Building up sufficient personal savings and investments for retirement will require a major shift in thinking. "Saving" may become the mantra of the 90s.

Retirement planning is much more, though, than just accumu-lating assets. As an estate planning attorney with nearly two decades of experience, I've seen in my practice the intercon-nected legal, health-related, family, and personal issues that are involved as well.

Baby Boomer Retirement is designed to make the process of planning for your retirement easier by guiding you through the three pillars of retirement planning as well as the main questions, fears, concerns, and decisions you need to address for yourself, your spouse, your children, and your parents.

Planning can save you money, stress and aggravation. Also, some opportunities will only be available if you've anticipated and mapped out a strategy in advance to deal with them.

The bottom line is that it's essential to start planning now. On the financial side alone, if you delay retirement planning by even 10 years, it may cost you three times as much each month to accumulate the same nest egg.

The goal of this book is to provide you with an understand-ing of the key issues so you can take the right steps now to protect your future and that of your loved ones.

BUILDING YOUR
NEST EGG

1.

Building a nest egg from scratch starting with the power of a piggy bank

There's a simple way you can start saving now even if you have enormous mortgage, personal and education costs.

Don't overlook the power of a piggy bank as a way to start a retirement and education savings plan.

It's painless to take your change each day and put it in a piggy bank or even a jar. Whether you earmark these coins for your children's college education or your own retirement (see No. 20 on pages 59 through 61 for the pros and cons of each approach), it's a simple step well worth taking.

The following example illustrates the financial power of piggy banks. Assume, starting at age 30, each evening you put that day's loose change in a piggy bank. If, on the average, you feed piggy 50¢ a day and also throw in an extra dollar every month, at the end of every three months, you'd have around $50 to invest. Ideally, you would put this money in an IRA or other retirement plan that would grow income tax free until distributions were taken out.

If that plan averages a 10% yearly return (which is the average growth for stocks since 1926), then at age 65, you'd have a retirement fund from your piggy bank of around $33,000. If every day you also add a dollar bill to your piggy bank, you'd have around $100,000 at age 65. Nice piggy.

2.

Preventing Social InSecurity

There are three sources you may be able to draw upon for retirement income: (1) your company's retirement plan, (2) your personal savings and investments, and (3) Social Security.

When you think of Social Security, you usually just think of retirement benefits. But Social Security may also provide an additional package of benefits to you and your family if you become severely disabled before retirement age or to your family upon your death. Social Security can thus provide an important base of *retirement*, *disability*, and *survivors* benefits for you *and* your family; however, don't rely solely on it.

Benefits could be hundreds of thousands of dollars

Most people underestimate the potential size of these benefits. The benefits could be worth hundreds of thousands of dollars to you and your loved ones.

For example, if you passed away in 1994, leaving a spouse and two young children (ages four and two), and your earnings were at the maximum Social Security levels, your family currently could receive around $28,000 per year for many years. Over the years, the family benefits could amount to hundreds of thousands of dollars. (If you want to see typical retirement, disability and survivor benefits, take a look at the tables on pages 173 and 174 in the Appendix.)

To avoid being shortchanged, you need to make sure Social Security has recorded your earnings correctly since it is *earnings* that determine the benefit amounts for you and your family members (which can include your spouse, ex-spouse, your children, step-children and, in some cases, even your dependent parents and grandchildren). And with more baby boomers having children later in life, don't forget to ask Social Security whether your children may be eligible to receive retirement benefits along with you.

When you or your family members apply for any of these possible Social Security benefits, how will you or they know if the benefits are based on the correct amount of your earnings? There is a simple way to find out and it costs one stamp every three years.

Form SSA-7004

To keep an eye on the information being used by Social Security, you need to complete a *Request for Earnings and Benefit Estimate Statement* (Form SSA-7004) at least every three years.

The form is free and it's easy to obtain (call 1/800-772-1213 to order the form). Then you just fill out the simple form and mail it to the Social Security Administration.

Social Security will mail a listing of your earnings (according to their records) and a projection of your Social Security retirement, disability and survivors benefits. You just need to compare one or two lines of your income tax returns with the benefit statement to determine whether the Social Security records are accurate. If there is any mistake in their records, you should have it corrected before it's too late.

How you can be shortchanged

Social Security has to deal with the earnings of every working person in the country every year. Do you think it's possible when keying in information for 100 million workers that a data entry operator ever leaves off a digit (thus changing $53,000 to $5,300) or reverses digits (changing $53,000 to $35,000)? It just may be your luck that you'll be the one this happens to. Even if Social Security never makes a mistake, could your company make one in sending in your earnings record? And, if you're a woman who has married and/or divorced and changed her name, have you advised Social Security of all name changes?

No problem, you say, since when the time rolls around to collect benefits, you'll double check everything. That's what you say. There are two problems with this reasoning.

First, in the year 2020 you probably won't be able to *find* your tax returns to verify your earnings from the 1990s. Second, and more important, even if you could locate those records, it could be too late under the law to make Social Security correct its records. The law makes it your responsibility to be sure Social Security records your earnings correctly. There are time limits for correcting errors. You may lose tremendous benefits for the rest of your life (and reduce your family's benefits, too) if a mistake is reported too late.

How long do you have to report a mistake?

In general, you have 3 years, 3 months, and 15 days after the year in which the earnings were earned or wages paid to report a needed correction. To correct 1995 earnings, you would need to notify Social Security no later than April 15, 1999. It might be possible to extend the correction period.

By 1999, Social Security will automatically send statements to all workers age 25 and over. However, don't wait for this to happen since you may lose the chance to correct earnings (and thus benefits) attributable to earlier periods. All it takes now is buying a stamp and spending a few minutes to protect the future of you and your family members.

3.

Keeping your employer in line: avoiding errors and problems with company retirement plans

Besides possible miscalculations in Social Security benefits just discussed on pages six to eight, don't overlook the possibility of mistakes occurring in your company's retirement plan (or your own plan if you are self-employed).

Even small errors can grow to significant dollar losses for you since the effects will compound over the years.

Again, many years from now in the 21st century, how will you be able to find and correct a mistake made in the prior century? The answer is, you won't, so monitor your plan as the years go by.

Get a summary plan description

First, get a summary plan description from your employer that tells you how retirement benefits are calculated. It's also a good idea to see such a description before you take on a new job and give up your current employment and retirement plan benefits.

Among the items to look for are: (1) whether bonuses, overtime and commissions are also included or is just your base salary used to determine retirement plan benefits; (2) whether employer contributions each year are based on a percentage of your salary that year or determined by a formula that also considers your age and the number of years you have until retirement; (3) whether your benefits at retirement (in the case of certain pension plans) are based on just your highest-earning years (no matter whether they were your first years on the job or your last) or just your last few years on the job (which may not be your highest-earning years, especially if commissions or bonuses are significant); (4) whether your time worked at sister companies is counted; and (5) how years of service are calculated if you take a pregnancy break or some other leave of absence (or even another job) and then come back.

Review your yearly statement

Every year you should receive a statement that summarizes the activity in your employer's retirement plan. You should check your statement for the following:

1. Are your salary, overtime, bonuses and commissions listed correctly?
2. Is the number of years you have worked at the company listed correctly?
3. Does the formula for company contributions and benefits on your behalf match up with your numbers and understanding?

For many of us, our employer's retirement plan may be more important than our Social Security benefits.

It's your money—so take time each year when you receive your employer's retirement plan statement to double check it.

4.

The secret way to save for retirement

The secret way to save for retirement is *not* to budget for it. If you try to budget a share for retirement savings, this item will always be at the bottom of the list since all other expenditures either have a more immediate, short-term benefit or may (inevitably) prove to be more urgent. Instead, you need to make the saving process so automatic that it doesn't require a conscious decision or act by you.

Automatic withdrawals from your paycheck or your checking account that go into a retirement plan or personal savings and investments can achieve this result. And with some retirement plans, there can be an added benefit of your contributions saving you income tax each year, too.

The sooner you set up an *automatic savings plan*, the more you'll have at retirement. A simple example shows the benefit of starting to save for retirement today.

Scenario One

At age 30, you put $2,000 into an IRA or other *tax-deferred* retirement plan (i.e., one that grows income-tax free until distributions are taken out). At ages 31 and 32, you also add $2,000 each year. Then, you stop making any contributions. If those three $2,000 contributions generate a return of 10% per year, then at age 65 you will have $140,000.

That's $140,000 from three $2,000 contributions.

Scenario Two

If, instead, you waited until age 45 to make your first $2,000 contribution and then you made $2,000 contributions religiously every year for the next 19 years under the same conditions as Scenario One, you would have only $114,000 at age 65.

Compound interest/compound growth

How can 20 contributions of $2,000 produce less than three contributions of $2,000? The answer is *compound interest* (also sometimes called *compound growth*).

Compound interest or compound growth refers to the effect over time of an investment growing in value *and* the reinvested growth also increasing over time. With a savings account, compound interest lets you receive interest on your interest. The longer you've invested, the greater the opportunity for compound interest or growth.

Compound interest is the reason why the earlier you start saving for retirement or your children's college education, the less you'll have to put away each month. With compound interest, once you've worked for your money, your money starts working for you.

Tax-deferred investments

There is a second component to successfully saving for retirement. If you use *tax-deferred investments* (e.g., IRAs, retirement plans and certain other investments) to save for retirement, you'll achieve your goal sooner.

A tax-deferred investment is one that isn't reduced by income tax while it is growing (income tax is paid later when distributions are taken out). It's no mystery why a tax-deferred investment grows faster than a non-deferred one. If the IRS suddenly announced you didn't have to pay income tax, your paycheck or profit would go up and you would have more money.

When you must pay income tax on increases in your investments during the growing years of a *non*-tax-deferred investment, it's like a baseball team with one or more of its players on the bench—you probably won't be able to cover all the bases.

So what's the lesson? Not that it's too late to start saving, but rather to invest as much as you can, as early as you can, to have the greatest opportunity for tax-deferred compound growth.

Many baby boomers utilize investments in stock *mutual funds* (i.e., companies with professional managers that pool your money with other investors to buy stocks) for building a nest egg. Mutual funds may or may not be tax-deferred, but most are set up and invested so that there is minimal income tax until you sell your shares—so the buildup of a non-tax-deferred mutual fund may approximate the performance of a tax-deferred fund. (Check with your accountant to see whether any particular mutual fund may result in more income tax than another.)

Ideally, you should arrange for automatic monthly payments to come off the top and go into a retirement account. If that isn't possible due to ever increasing financial demands, then whenever you get a bonus, raise or refund, why not take all or a portion of that windfall to open up or add to your retirement fund?

If you delay, you will pay!

5.

Avoiding ten common errors

You may prevent ten mistakes that frequently occur in retirement planning by taking the following steps:

1. Maximize contributions to *tax-deferred* retirement plans (see page 12).

2. Diversify investments (don't put all of your nest eggs in the same basket).

3. Consider the effects of inflation (see page 24).

4. Assess your risk comfort level.

5. Avoid a risky investment that promises too big a profit.

6. Select your financial advisor very carefully.

7. Calculate the effects of income taxes, including taxes due on early withdrawals of investments.

8. Consider non-tax costs of investments (e.g., high fees if you want to bail out early from an annuity; lack of liquidity so that it's difficult to get your money out of a limited partnership; or high annual management costs with some mutual funds).

9. Take the time and effort to monitor how your investments are doing (even if you have a financial advisor).

10. Start saving for retirement as soon as possible.

6.

How to select a financial advisor

Will you spend more time thinking about the topping for your next pizza than you will in selecting a financial advisor?

Among the questions you should *ask yourself* are:

1. Does my accountant know and recommend a good financial advisor?

2. Do I know other clients who have worked with the advisor for at least several years?

   Ideally, you would answer "yes" to each of these questions but a "yes" to either one may be sufficient.

Among the questions you should *ask the prospective advisor* are:

1. Am I like your typical client?

2. What are your qualifications and length of experience?

3. How will you be compensated? Will you earn a fee *(a)* on commissions for selling investments, *(b)* a fee for services but no commissions, or *(c)* a combination of a fee and commissions? Is your fee a flat fee including all services or is it calculated on an hourly basis at a specified hourly rate?

   All things being equal, the fee with no commission, option *(b)*, should result in the most objective advice for you.

4. Will you let me see financial plans of other clients like me with the client names blocked out?

The *prospective financial advisor should ask you* at least the following questions:

1. What are your financial and personal goals, short-term and long-term?

2. How much risk are you willing to take on investments?

3. What are your needs for cash besides what is invested in long-term investments?

The *financial advisor should do* at least the following:

1. Fully explain, verbally and in writing, a probable game plan for the next year as well as the next 3, 5, 10, and 20 years.

2. Fully explain, verbally and in writing, a proposed investment and wait for you to feel comfortable with it before having you plunk your money down.

3. Welcome questions from you and provide easily understood answers.

Where to find a financial advisor

There are a lot of people out there who want to give you financial advice. How can you determine the qualifications of a good financial advisor? A good place to start is to ask your accountant and attorney. You may want someone who has earned the designation of Certified Financial Planner (CFP) or Chartered Financial Consultant (ChFC).

And, remember, an advisor recommends investments geared to meeting *your* objectives—not the other way around.

7.

When to start building your nest egg

We're all on a journey headed for retirement. You can be a tortoise or a hare but you may end up needing to be a cheetah if you don't start saving for retirement now.

It's really not a question of when to start building your nest egg. If you are a baby boomer, you should have *already* started. It's really how much do you need to save each year once you get serious about building your nest egg.

To have a comfortable retirement, you generally need between 60 and 100% of your pre-retirement annual income.

You will not be able to retire just on Social Security benefits. For most people, Social Security will supply about 20 to 40% of pre-retirement income.

If Social Security supplies about 20% of your needed retirement income, where will you get the balance to have 60 to 100% of your pre-retirement annual income? There are four possible sources:

1. Your company's retirement plan (or your own plan if you're self-employed)

2. Your personal savings and investments

3. Working in retirement (this could take the fun out of retiring)

4. Receiving an inheritance (don't count on one since you never know what financial and health problems are

ahead for a person who plans to leave you an inheritance).

Five factors affecting the starting date

The amount of time you have to build your nest egg depends upon five key factors:

1. The earlier you want to retire, the more you need to save now.

   The sooner you retire, the less time you have to accumulate a nest egg. That means you need to save more each year. Also, when you retire earlier, you are giving up a salary and extra years of contributions to retirement plans and dipping into your nest egg sooner.

2. The later you start saving for retirement, the more you need to save each year once you get started. Your savings will have less time to grow through compound interest.

3. The higher the percentage of pre-retirement annual income you want for retirement (e.g, 100% rather than 60%), the more you need to save now.

4. The longer you'll live in retirement, the more you need to save now.

   The size of a nest egg that needs to last until age 95 has to be larger than one to last to age 75.

5. The higher the inflation rate in the future, the more you need to save now.

8.

The benefit of a good foundation

As you'll see in the following example and table, if you already have a retirement plan with one year's salary in it, it will be far easier for you to accumulate your desired nest egg.

Let's look at 10 friends who all want their nest eggs to produce 70% of their pre-retirement annual income. Each of them expects Social Security to supply 20% of their 70% goal, leaving them with the job of funding the 50% difference (70% goal less 20% from Social Security). They each expect to live 30 years in retirement. They're all assuming that the growth on their nest egg savings until they retire will outpace inflation by 6% per year (i.e., if inflation is 3%, then their investments will earn 9%, which is 6% more than the 3% inflation).

The table shown below gives a rough estimate of the percentage of salary each friend needs to save each year if the friend (1) had no current savings and (2) had retirement savings equal to one year's salary.

No. of years to retirement	Percentage of salary to save if no savings	Percentage of salary to save with one year's salary in savings
10	60%	47%
15	30%	21%
20	22%	13%
25	15%	8%
30	10%	3%

See how this table applies to these 10 friends—5 of them with no current savings and the other 5 with retirement savings equal to one year's salary.

10 years to save until retirement

Al and Jasmine want to retire in 10 years. Al needs to save 60% of his salary each year for the next 10 years because he has no savings. Jasmine needs to save 47% of her salary each year because she has already saved one year of her salary. Al and Jasmine feel they either need to find a magic genie or inherit from a king to reach their goals.

15 years to save until retirement

Ralph and Alice want to retire in 15 years. Ralph needs to save 30% of his salary each year for the next 15 years because he has no savings. Alice needs to save 21% of her salary each year because she has savings equal to one year of salary. When Alice told Ralph how much more he needed to save than her, he said "to the moon, Alice, to the moon."

20 years to save until retirement

Ben and Jerry want to retire in 20 years. Ben needs to save 22% of his salary each year for the next 20 years because he has no savings. Jerry needs to save 13% of his salary each year because he has savings equal to one year of salary. Ben and Jerry took another look and decided they already have enough to retire now. It's the other Ben and Jerry who have to keep working for 20 years.

25 years to save until retirement

Thelma and Louise want to retire in 25 years. Thelma needs to save 15% of her salary each year for the next 25 years because she has no savings. Louise needs to save 8% of her salary each year because she has savings equal to one year of salary. Thelma and Louise are reconsidering whether they'll live 25 years before retiring, let alone 30 years in retirement.

30 years to save until retirement

Bill and Hillary want to retire in 30 years. Bill needs to save 10% of his salary each year for the next 30 years because he has no savings. Hillary needs to save 3% of her salary each year because she has savings equal to one year of salary. Hillary has mixed feelings that she'll be able to invest her money in a conservative manner and still reach her goal.

Summary

The benefit of having one year's salary in savings or in a retirement plan is tremendous. It can greatly reduce the amount and percentage of salary to save each year during the remaining years until retirement. Again, it's the power of compound interest that makes the difference.

9.

Learning new retirement math: how to calculate the right-size nest egg

Now that you see the wisdom in saving for retirement, you need to learn some new math—"new retirement math," that is.

New retirement math is calculating how much you'll need to accumulate between your company's retirement plan and your personal savings and investments by your retirement date in order to supplement Social Security retirement benefits and live out the rest of your life in comfort and security. If you can't stand looking at any numbers, then at the very least remember this general rule for building the right-size nest egg: you should save *no less* than 10% of your income every year.

How to calculate the right-size nest egg

There are, however, calculations and financial projections you (and your financial advisor) should do to pinpoint the size of your nest egg. You need to know what's behind the numbers.

Every financial projection is a series of assumptions. A small change in an assumption such as the future rate of return (growth) or the inflation rate can have dramatic effects. Whenever you review a financial projection, ask the preparer of the data whether the preparer used "optimistic," "pessimistic" or "realistic" assumptions. Always ask to see separate calculations based on these three types of assumptions.

Translating this to nest egg planning you should see different calculations with a range of different assumptions such as:

1. A long-term annual rate of return of 4%, 6%, 8%, 10%, and 12%
2. An inflation rate of 4%, 6%, and 8%
3. Retirement income equal to 60%, 80%, and 100% of pre-retirement income
4. Your income staying the same until retirement, going up 2% or 4% per year
5. A retirement age of 62, 65, 67, or 70
6. Life span after retirement of 10, 15, 20, 25, 30, 35, or 40 years
7. No inheritance by retirement age or a possible inheritance based upon your parents' asset situation.

Although there are tables on pages 26 and 27 to show you sample calculations to reach desired nest eggs, it doesn't do you a service to let you think any one table has the right answer for you.

You and/or your financial advisor should ideally use the computer program listed in the Appendix (or a similar program) to do different nest egg calculations using variable assumptions to pinpoint your needs.

How can you predict the future of the economy?

Even though no one can predict the future, we usually look to the past in trying to decide what inflation, interest rates and rates of return on investments will be like down the road. We get a certain comfort in knowing history, including financial history, which helps us make educated guesses about the future.

The Great Depression started in 1929. If you look at investment returns since 1926, three years before the start of the Depression, there are some interesting results.

During the almost 70 years since 1926, stocks have averaged a compounded annual return of about 10%. During the same period, long-term interest rates and bonds have averaged about half of that.

Within any given year as well as any 10-year period, each of these types of investments has often suffered tremendous losses as well as enjoyed startling gains. To a lesser degree, the first half of 1994 saw stocks lose about 6% in value while certificates of deposit generated about a 2% positive return.

Every financial projection for retirement benefits and education costs in this book (and outside of it) is just an estimate but is based on observations about the past.

Effect of inflation

Let's see how different assumptions about rates of inflation could affect your nest egg.

Inflation has averaged 4% over the last 40 years. Over the last 25 years, it has averaged almost 6%.

After 18 years of 4% per year inflation, a dollar is worth just 50¢. After 36 years of 4% per year inflation, a dollar is worth just 25¢.

After 18 years of 8% per year inflation, a dollar is worth just 25¢. After 36 years of 8% per year inflation, a dollar is worth just 6¢.

If your income and resources do not grow with inflation, your buying power will be diminished to a substantial degree.

Effect of an inheritance

There will be an unprecedented transfer of wealth from the parents of baby boomers. However, any given boomer does not know:

1. What financial roadblocks may affect the size of that inheritance, including financial reverses suffered by parents and high nursing home or other medical costs for parents

2. Who will be named as your parent(s)' beneficiaries (if you are married, you and your spouse may be assuming that there will be two inheritances; however, if your spouse passes away before your in-laws, it's quite likely that your spouse's parents will not include you in their will or trust)

3. What death tax costs will be at that time.

However, if you do receive an inheritance by retirement age (but don't count on it), the size of the nest egg for you to accumulate and your corresponding monthly savings goal will be smaller.

Nest egg examples

Keeping in mind that no set of assumptions is guaranteed to be correct, take a look at how some "realistic" assumptions would apply to baby boomers ages 30, 35, 40 and 45 starting to save today for retirement to supplement Social Security benefits: (1) the goal is retirement income equal to 80% of pre-retirement income, including Social Security retirement benefits; (2) investments are to be put in a tax-deferred retirement plan (see pages 12 and 13) which will grow faster than taxable personal savings and investments; (3) the annual rate of return (growth) is 10%, which is the average since 1926 in the stock market; (4) inflation is 5.3% (the average for the last 30 years); (5) retirement age of 66 to 67 (the Social Security retirement age for baby boomers is not age 65—see No. 19 on page 53; (6) average life expectancy to age 90; (7) there is *no* current company retirement plan *or* personal savings and investments (any amounts already on hand can significantly reduce the yearly amount to save); and (8) no inheritance from parents is expected (an inheritance can reduce the yearly amount to save, too).

The last column in the following table shows the yearly amount to save to reach the 80% goal through a tax-deferred retirement plan (there are limitations on annual contributions to retirement plans which should be reviewed with your tax advisor) or equivalent tax-deferred personal savings and investments.

Your age today	Your salary now	Retirement goal = 80% current salary	% of salary to save	Yearly amount to save
30	$30,000	$24,000	4.9%	$ 1,470
35	$30,000	$24,000	6.5%	$ 1,950
40	$30,000	$24,000	10.8%	$ 3,240
45	$30,000	$24,000	15.2%	$ 4,560
30	$40,000	$32,000	5.8%	$ 2,320
35	$40,000	$32,000	8.0%	$ 3,200
40	$40,000	$32,000	12.6%	$ 5,040
45	$40,000	$32,000	18.4%	$ 7,360
30	$50,000	$40,000	6.9%	$ 3,450
35	$50,000	$40,000	9.1%	$ 4,550
40	$50,000	$40,000	14.4%	$ 7,200
45	$50,000	$40,000	20.8%	$10,400
30	$60,000	$48,000	7.4%	$ 4,440
35	$60,000	$48,000	10.0%	$ 6,000
40	$60,000	$48,000	15.6%	$ 9,360
45	$60,000	$48,000	22.4%	$13,440
30	$70,000	$56,000	8.2%	$ 5,740
35	$70,000	$56,000	11.0%	$ 7,700
40	$70,000	$56,000	17.0%	$11,900
45	$70,000	$56,000	24.6%	$17,220

Your age today	Your salary now	Retirement goal = 80% current salary	% of salary to save	Yearly amount to save
30	$80,000	$64,000	8.8%	$ 7,040
35	$80,000	$64,000	11.9%	$ 9,520
40	$80,000	$64,000	18.2%	$14,560
45	$80,000	$64,000	26.2%	$20,960
30	$90,000	$72,000	9.3%	$ 8,370
35	$90,000	$72,000	12.6%	$11,340
40	$90,000	$72,000	19.2%	$17,280
45	$90,000	$72,000	27.5%	$24,750
30	$100,000	$80,000	9.8%	$ 9,800
35	$100,000	$80,000	13.2%	$13,200
40	$100,000	$80,000	19.9%	$19,900
45	$100,000	$80,000	28.5%	$28,500

Note on the table that the younger you are when you start your saving, the less you need to save each year. Also, the more you earn, the greater the percentage of salary you need to save to attain your retirement goal.

During retirement, you may decide to borrow against or sell your house, which can reduce the amount you need to save each year before retirement.

10.

The 20-minute budget

Since everyone hates to budget and most people that do budget don't stick to it, there has to be a better way to get you to stare your financial situation in the face—the 20-minute budget.

Take a sheet of paper and draw a line down the middle. On the left side of the paper, list your estimated monthly income from all sources. Then, deduct the automatic payments you want to make to (1) save for retirement and (2) save for your children's college education. What's left after these deductions becomes your new monthly income. By taking retirement and college education expenses off first, you will be able to budget for these items. It's just everything else that may be a problem.

On the right side of the paper, list your average monthly expenses by category. Subtract the total of these expenses from the monthly net income and you'll see how much play you have left in your money (or whether you're played out). Then pretend you are not a congressperson and you must actually balance your budget. See what you can cut out or reduce on the expense side until you can balance your budget. Short of getting an extra job to boost the income side of the ledger, you might want to take a closer look at your debt to see if there are ways to reduce cost there.

How to make one dollar grow into two

You may have to earn two pre-tax dollars to produce one after-tax dollar. In other words, two dollars of earnings can shrink down to one dollar in hand after the payment of federal and state (and city) income taxes as well as Social Security/self-employment tax.

So, if you can find a way to *save* a dollar, it might be the same as increasing your income by two dollars.

The "36% return" on your investment

You may have debt on which interest is not deductible (such as personal credit card interest). If you are paying 18% interest on unpaid balances, do you need to earn 36% on your investments or earn the equivalent wages to wind up with the money to pay the 18% interest? It will depend on your income tax bracket but the bottom line is no matter what income tax bracket you are in, you are paying off credit card interest with after-tax, non-deductible dollars.

It may be wiser to take out a home equity loan to pay off credit card debts so the interest portion of your payments qualifies for an income tax deduction (check with your tax advisor since not all home equity loans qualify for this deduction).

Before seeing a home equity loan as a cure-all, remember, that if you default on a home equity loan, you may lose your house.

You may instead want to shop around for another credit card with a lower interest rate. Before you switch, make sure you understand whether the lower rate is only for a limited time period. If so, you might get stuck with much higher rates after the introductory lower rate period. Also, if you are counting on the lower rate applying to prior charges that are being transferred over to a new card, make sure that this indeed is the case. Otherwise, the new rate may only apply to new charges. Pay as much as you can each month to reduce the amount as well as the accompanying tension.

You may also want to consider refinancing the loan on your house to lower your monthly payments. Before taking this step, make sure that you consider (1) the costs vs. the benefits especially if you'll want or have to sell your house within a few years of the refinancing and (2) whether you are adding additional years for the payback of your loan. Also see No. 31 on page 91 and No. 40 on page 106.

Prioritize your money

You need to prioritize your monthly investments between retirement planning, educational expenses and high-interest, non-deductible debt. Your best investment may be to pay off debt first since you may not find an investment that pays as much as your debt costs you. And the bonus to this strategy is that less debt means less stress.

11.

Seven ways to make sure your retirement investments are right for you

You should not skimp in spending for a crystal ball to predict the future of your investments. If you find it difficult to get an accurate crystal ball then (1) seek qualified professional advice; (2) cross-check the advice you are given with another financial advisor including your accountant; (3) listen to your gut—if you feel uneasy, the advice you are getting may be wrong, or at least, wrong for you; (4) be prepared to meet people who will promise you the moon but take you to the cleaners instead; and (5) educate yourself. The more reading you do, the better equipped you'll be to avoid costly surprises. So, what are you to do?

Here are seven ways to make sure your retirement investments are right for you:

1. First, determine your pre-retirement and retirement goals and objectives (e.g., how important is it for you to own a house right now, before retirement?)

2. Then, prioritize those retirement goals and objectives with your other goals. Since there is never enough money to satisfy all our needs and desires, you need to know what's most important to you, now and in the long run.

3. Think about how much risk you are willing (and need) to take on to meet your retirement goals and objectives. Take a peek at the worst-case scenario for each alter-

native. When you review alternative investment choices, pretend you've made the investment before you actually do so and see if it results in sleepless nights.

4. Diversify your investments so all of your nest eggs are not in one basket. Usually, it's not a good idea to buy just a few stocks, or invest in just one mutual fund—it's too easy for your entire financial future to go sour this way.

5. Consider the income tax impact before making a decision (check with your accountant).

6. Don't let your retirement investments get eaten up by inflation, which can gobble up your investment as well as any growth on your investment.

7. Before you make an investment, get professional advice and understand what the cost will be to get out of it if you conclude the investment was a mistake.

12.

How to take years off your mortgage payments

If you just bought a house or refinanced it, there is a good chance that you have a mortgage that will take nearly another 30 years to be paid off. How old will you be in 30 years? Do you still want to be making mortgage payments at age 65, 70 or 78?

There are two easy ways to avoid 30 years of mortgage payments. One way is to take out a 15-year loan. With a 15-year loan, you're making higher monthly payments for 15 years (usually at a higher interest rate, about ½% above the rate on a 30-year loan). This type of loan commits you to higher monthly payments throughout the 15 years.

The advantage of a 15-year loan as compared to a 30-year loan is that the *total interest paid* by you is much *lower* since your loan will be paid off in half the time (compare examples one and four on page 35).

Another way to pay your loan off sooner

Another way to save interest, but have greater flexibility as to the amount of your monthly payment, is to have a 30-year loan and make extra payments in an amount you determine. A small but regular extra payment can result in your saving interest payments equal to 50% or more of the original loan amount.

There are two main questions you need to ask yourself in deciding whether to pay off your loan early. First, what is the financial benefit or detriment of paying off your loan early? Second, what is the psychological benefit you'll receive if your home is debt-free at retirement age or earlier?

Financial considerations

If your house is not worth much more than your loan, it may not be a good idea to pay extra money on the loan.

If you do not pay off your mortgage early, you will probably get an income tax benefit from deducting the mortgage interest on your income tax return. This reduces the real cost of your mortgage payments. Have your accountant explain the income tax rules that may limit, however, the actual benefit of mortgage interest deductions, especially with refinanced loans.

If you do not pay off your loan early, you will have more money to invest. But will you invest that money to receive a greater benefit than paying off your loan early?

If you pay off your loan early, will too much of your net worth be tied up in your house, which is an illiquid asset (i.e., hard to turn into cash immediately)? Also see No. 31 on page 91 and No. 40 on page 106 for additional information.

If you have a 30-year loan, there are three ways to make extra payments to reduce the length (and cost) of your 30-year loan. One way, the hardest way, is to come up with one extra monthly payment each year so that you actually make 13 monthly payments per year instead of 12 payments per year. A second way that may be available through your lender is to let you make payments every two weeks so you still end up making 13 monthly payments but you do it through 26 bi-weekly payments. The third way is just to pay something extra every month (e.g., $100) with your regular mortgage payment, ideally through an automatic withdrawal from your checking account. That reduces your principal balance by that extra amount ($100) per month.

The following four examples show the effect of various payment schedules and assume that there is a $100,000 fixed-rate loan that is taken out (or refinanced) when you are 40 years old.

Example One: 30-year loan at 8% interest with no extra payments

360 payments (30 years times 12 payments per year) of $734 each for a total of **$264,240** ($100,000 principal plus $164,240 interest paid on the loan).

Example Two: 30-year loan at 8% interest with no extra principal payments but with payments made bi-weekly rather than once a month

593 payments (22 5/6 years times 26 payments per year) of $367 each for a total of **$217,844** ($100,000 principal plus $117,844 interest paid on the loan).

Example Three: 30-year loan at 8% interest with extra $100 principal payment each month

240 payments (20 years times 12 payments per year) of $834 each (the extra $100 going to reduce the principal due) for a total of **$200,160** ($100,000 principal and $100,160 interest) paid on the loan.

Example Four: 15-year loan with no extra principal payments at 8½% interest (the interest rate is usually ½% higher with a 15-year loan)

180 payments (15 years times 12 payments per year) of $985 each for a total of **$177,300** ($100,000 principal plus $77,300 interest) paid on the loan.

Summary:

Example One: For 30 years at $734 per month with no extra principal payments, you'll pay $264,240 to age 70.

Example Two: For 22 5/6 years at $367 every two weeks, you'll pay $217,844 to age 63 and save almost $50,000 in interest payments as compared to Example One.

Example Three: For 20 years at $834 per month, you'll pay $200,160 to age 60 and save over $60,000 in interest payments as compared to Example One.

Example Four: For 15 years at $985 per month with no extra principal payments, you'll pay $177,300 to age 55 and save almost $90,000 in interest payments as compared to Example One.

This summary illustrates how compound interest can work against you (i.e., 30-year loans) just as it can work for you in saving for retirement in a tax-deferred plan.

Some loans have penalties if you pay them off early (*prepayment penalties*). Even loans that have prepayment penalties usually allow you to pay off a certain amount each year without being subject to the penalty. Have your attorney check your loan documents on this matter.

Psychological considerations

In balancing the financial pros and cons, remember that a mortgage reduction plan offers the psychological advantage of making your mortgage go away faster and that can be worth a lot.

13.

The federally insured surprise: retirement assets in banks may not be fully federally insured

You probably know that mutual funds are *not* federally insured. When you invest in a mutual fund, you are depending upon your common sense and governmental regulators to be sure any given fund is kept in line.

However, you may think that *all* retirement funds in banks are *completely* federally insured. Not so. The maximum federal insurance limit on bank deposits for IRAs, Keogh plans, and 401(k) plans is currently $100,000. That's $100,000 total per bank and not $100,000 per type of plan.

Whether you have one or more of these types of plans, you should always confirm the Federal Deposit Insurance Corporation limit for your funds in bank accounts. The solution currently is to keep under the $100,000 FDIC limit in any one institution.

Even if you do not have $100,000 in retirement funds in a bank now, you might in the future. And even if you never will have $100,000 in such plans, you still could be affected if the regulations lower the insured limit in the future. There are also rules on the $100,000 limitation for non-retirement accounts, too. So, at least every year, have your banker confirm the federally insured limits for your retirement plans and other accounts at the bank.

14.

Seven ways to reduce your income taxes

Since no one likes to pay income tax on top of Social Security tax, it makes sense to take a look at ways to help minimize income taxes.

One: Invest in qualified retirement plans

Consider sheltering your income and the return on your investments by investing in qualified retirement plans. Also, if your employer offers matching contributions in a 401(k) plan, for example, don't overlook this opportunity as the best bang for your buck.

Two: Maximize tax-free income

The higher your income tax bracket, the less you pocket on taxable income such as bank interest and stock dividends. It may pay for you to switch a portion of your investments into tax-free income such as municipal bonds. Tax-free means the income is not subject to income tax.

For example, if you're in a 39.6% income tax bracket, a 4.5% *tax-free* investment can net more than a 6.62% *taxable* investment. What this means is that a 6.62% return on an investment taxable at the 39.6% bracket is the same as a 4% return on a tax-free investment. Before you lock into such investments, you should ask your tax advisor about all the tax and financial ramifications of taking such a course of action.

*Three: Avoid having tax-free investments in tax-deferred
    retirement plans*

Generally, tax-free investments (such as *municipal bonds*) earn
less than taxable investments. The reason is that you are
receiving an additional benefit due to the income being free
from income tax (federal, state, or both as the case may be).

Income inside a tax-deferred retirement plan or annuity grows
free of income tax anyway. Income tax is paid when distributions are taken out of the plan or annuity.

So, all things considered, you do not want to have lower-
return tax-free investments inside a tax-deferred retirement
plan or annuity since your investments will earn less with no
compensating tax benefit.

Four: Consider variable annuities

If you have maxed out your retirement plan opportunities,
you should consider *variable annuities* and other tax-free
choices. With your left-over taxable dollars (if there are any),
you can invest in a way that allows growth without income
tax until distributions are taken. There is no limit on how
much you can invest but you will not receive an income tax
deduction for the contributions you make to the annuity. You
are using after-tax dollars to fund such an investment. It's
risky, though, because if the investments don't work out, your
annuity will be reduced accordingly.

This type of investment might also be wise when you are
receiving Social Security benefits because the growth inside
the annuity isn't being counted as income in calculating the
income tax on Social Security benefits.

Before you go ahead with such annuities, however, discuss
with your tax and financial advisor whether investing in stock
mutual funds outside of a variable annuity would produce a

better result. Gains from mutual funds that are invested in stocks qualify for the 28% federal capital gains tax as compared to the potentially higher ordinary income tax rate on annuity payouts. On the other hand, your income tax bracket may be lower at the time you cash in your annuities. Also, remember that annuities usually have charges ("forfeitures") if you cancel ("surrender") the policy before many years have gone by. See No. 16 on page 44 for a definition and further discussion of annuities.

Five: Maximize capital gain income

Federal income tax on gain from *ordinary income* can be as high as 39.6%. Compare this to the 28% maximum federal income tax on *capital gains*.

An example of ordinary income would be dividends on stocks or interest on savings or bonds. This type of income, under current federal income tax law, can be taxed at 39.6%.

An example of capital gain would be the growth in value of a stock over more than a year's time. This growth, under current federal income tax law, cannot be taxed at more than 28% after a sale. Since capital gain income (e.g., gain on the sale of stocks) is taxed at a lower federal income tax rate than interest or dividend income, consider investments that produce capital gain income. However, first talk to your accountant and/or financial advisor about how the government may tax such gain under the *alternative minimum tax*.

Six: Consider a stepped-up basis before you sell assets

Assume you are very ill and are considering selling assets to make things simpler for your heirs. There could be a tremendous amount of pent-up capital gain in your assets (e.g., a rental house or stock you paid $50,000 for is now worth $200,000). If you sell now, there is income tax to pay on the gain. If, instead, your heirs inherit the assets and they sell the assets, their starting point for federal income tax gain or loss is what the assets were worth on the date of your death (e.g., $200,000 in this example). The difference can amount to tens or hundreds of thousands of dollars in unnecessary income tax from a sale during your lifetime.

Seven: Improve your record keeping

There are two main areas for which you'll want to keep financial records on investments: (1) improvements to your residence that reduce the amount of income tax when you sell your house (see page 161) and (2) stock fund investments.

With stock fund investments, better records can reduce income tax gain by allowing you to track which portion of your investment can be sold to produce the least amount of gain and which portion has already been taxed (e.g., capital gain distributions that are reinvested).

15.

Saving taxes on distributions from retirement plans

Distributions from retirement plans can be subject to income, death and excise taxes. There are usually ways to minimize the impact of all of these taxes if steps are taken in advance to plan for them.

Avoiding unnecessary income tax

If you aren't careful, you'll pay an unnecessary 20% income tax on a retirement plan distribution you intended to *roll over* (i.e., put into another qualified retirement plan).

This tax very often comes about if your employer is down-sizing (or now euphemistically known as "right-sizing") and your retirement benefits are transferred out of your former employer's retirement plan. Your employer might ask you a simple question, "Do you want the money sent directly to you?" and innocently enough you respond, "Sure." You can, in fact, avoid this tax by not touching the retirement plan distribution even for an instant.

Instead, have the distribution go directly into an IRA rollover or another *qualified plan* (see if the new employer's plan allows you to do so from day one on the job).

If, instead, your retirement plan benefits are distributed directly to you and you, in turn, immediately put the distribution into an IRA or your new employer's plan, the IRS requires 20% of the distribution to be withheld from you (and paid to the IRS). In addition to this 20% withholding, you may have to pay income tax on the withheld portion (plus a 10% penalty if you are under age 59½). Always get professional advice before retirement benefits are distributed.

Rules for withdrawal of retirement funds. You may have a choice as to whether your retirement plan benefits are paid out to you in one lump sum or over a period of time (or for the duration of your life or until both you and your spouse pass away). Each type of distribution has income tax consequences. In some cases, you may be able to reduce the income tax due on distributions if you make a special "income tax election" on your income tax return. Ask your accountant about the alternatives available to you.

Beneficiary designations. Talk to your accountant and attorney about how you should complete your beneficiary designation forms to save and/or defer income, death and excise taxes on retirement plan distributions.

How to take money out early and avoid penalties

Generally, early withdrawals (before age 59½) from retirement plans and IRAs are subject to a penalty. However, you may need to take money out of a retirement plan before age 59½. Ask your accountant whether you can avoid the penalty under an exception or by a withdrawal payout schedule tied to your life expectancy.

16.

Living long and in comfort: look to annuities

Besides trying to predict long-term investment returns and inflation rates, baby boomers need to make some educated guesses about their life expectancy and future health condition. How long are you going to live? To age 75? 85? 95? 105?

Have you planned for your money to last as long you do? If not, you should consider investing in an *annuity*.

An annuity is a contract to pay you an amount of money for a specified period of time. It's very often a promise by an insurance company to pay you as long as you live.

Even if you have a company retirement plan, personal savings and investments and Social Security to count on, you may want to supplement your retirement income with an annuity.

The difference between an annuity and a nest egg

There's a difference between building up a retirement nest egg and having an annuity that will pay as long as you live.

In the past, many company pension plans provided employees with a guaranteed annuity that was a percentage of the employee's salary (i.e., it lasted an employee's lifetime and possibly for the lifetime of the spouse of the employee as well). This made it easier for retirees to plan for the future.

During the last decade, employers have tended to drop these pension plans and instead have substituted 401(k) plans. 401(k) plans don't provide an annuity related to a percentage of your salary—instead they allow for a tax-deferred buildup of a nest egg and it's anyone's guess as to how long that nest egg will last in retirement.

401(k) plans call for *the employees* to pay all or most of the contributions to the plans. A 401(k) plan has no definite time span as far as payouts—it might last your lifetime or it may run out during your lifetime.

A danger with 401(k) plans is their accessibility—you can borrow against or withdraw money from the plans too easily so that in some cases your retirement plan may retire before you do. 401(k) plans are good to have—it's just that you might need to supplement the plans with an investment that will be around the rest of your life, such as an annuity.

If you do take out a loan under your 401(k) plan, check with your accountant as to whether the interest on the loan will be deductible on your income tax return and with your attorney as to the other consequences of such a loan.

How should you approach purchasing an annuity? First, see if you have a need for an annuity as part of your retirement planning. If the answer is yes, then you should talk to at least two qualified professionals about annuities. Annuities come in many shapes and sizes. Usually they are sold by insurance companies through agents, stockbrokerage houses or banks. Have the professionals critique each other's proposed annuities (at no cost to you).

Do you need an annuity?

Your need for an annuity at retirement will depend upon the composition of your assets, your personal circumstances, income flow, expenses, life span and future health status, and inflation at that time.

At retirement age, perhaps your biggest expense through the years, your mortgage, will be behind you. But will nursing home expenses be the substitute? (See No. 41 and No. 42 on pages 109 through 116 for ways to insure for these expenses.)

Usually, the following expenses go down in retirement: mortgage, personal debts, income and Social Security taxes, life and disability insurance (which are very often discontinued), medical insurance, food, clothing, furniture, and transportation.

Usually, the following expenses go up in retirement: property taxes and rent, house repairs/maintenance, long-term care insurance, and vacation/travel expenses.

Anatomy of an annuity

Annuities, like many investments, can be complex. Since we all can hear sales presentations differently, you should always get a written summary spelling out the critical elements of any proposed annuity before signing on the dotted line.

Since this is an investment that is to last a lifetime, it's very important that the company issuing the annuity (which is a promise to pay you money) be of sound financial strength. There are various rating services (Best, Moody's, Standard & Poors, Weiss Research and Duff & Phelps) that rank insurance companies according to their financial integrity and claims paying record. You should always see these ratings.

There are other factors to consider, too.

How long will the annuity last? Will the annuity pay *(a)* to age 65, *(b)* as long as you live, *(c)* a fixed term (e.g. 10 years), or *(d)* a combination of the above (e.g., for your life but no less than 10 years so that if you die early into the distribution period, your heirs will receive up to 10 years' worth of payments)?

Some annuities allow early withdrawals without any forfeiture if (1) rates of return fall below a certain minimum, (2) you withdraw no more than a certain percentage (e.g., 10%) per calendar year, or (3) you enter a nursing home—please note that the IRS would not be as forgiving and would charge you a penalty for an early withdrawal for any of these reasons (check with your accountant).

Although annuities can be used to help fund long-term nursing care costs, a *fixed-rate annuity* (see below for a definition) may not produce enough income, depending upon inflation's effect on nursing home costs. On the flip side, you should also check with your attorney concerning the possible effect of an annuity on your qualifying for long-term governmental nursing home assistance.

Next, take a look at the various types of annuities available to you.

Fixed-rate annuities

A more conservative annuity to consider is a fixed-rate annuity. It resembles both a certificate of deposit and a non-deductible IRA.

It's like a certificate of deposit in that you usually receive a guaranteed rate for a period of time such as one year. After the guarantee period, the rate of return rises or falls according to interest rate changes in the economy, but there is usually a guaranteed minimum or floor that you'll receive even if interest rates go down dramatically.

It's like an IRA in that the earnings grow tax-deferred until they are taken out and distributed. And like an IRA, there are penalties for early withdrawals and you pay income tax on withdrawals. But better than an IRA, there is no limit on how much money you can put into the annuity.

There are fixed-rate annuities where you only make one payment (i.e., a *single premium annuity*) or where you can make many payments (i.e., *flexible annuity*).

So what can go wrong with these annuities? First, they are not federally insured. You need to look to the soundness of the company issuing the annuity before plunking down your money.

Second, if you change your mind and want to end the annuity early, you may be facing income tax, penalties, and early withdrawal penalties imposed by the issuer of the annuity.

So, the fine print needs to be checked to see what you'd have left in case you wanted to get out of the annuity early. And that raises the question as to how many customers do walk away from a particular company's annuity. Take a look at the numbers to see what percentage of customers renew their annuity. Is the percentage low because the company offers a great return for the first year and then the return drops significantly? You should consult your attorney, accountant, life insurance salesperson, and financial planner before signing on the dotted line.

Variable annuities

If you are open to more risk and more opportunity, you might consider a *variable annuity*. Unlike a fixed annuity, however, with a variable annuity you might lose all of your investment. Usually, you are using this type of annuity to invest in stocks or mutual funds in a way that shelters the gain from income tax until the monies are withdrawn.

Just like non-deductible IRAs, there's no limit on how much you can put into these annuities and the income tax is deferred until you make withdrawals. Likewise, early withdrawals are subject to penalties. But, one advantage, as with IRAs, is that you can switch your investments around within the different mutual funds offered through the annuity without subjecting yourself to income tax.

As with any mutual fund, the best track record for the future is the past track record. The longer the track record, the better the indication of how the fund will fare in good times and lean. (However, past performance is no guarantee of future performance.)

When you are comparing the returns on the choice of funds within an annuity, also look at the fees, costs, and charges that are imposed to come up with a realistic view of possible future performance.

17.

How to do good and increase your cash flow

You can actually increase your income and cash flow for life by giving assets to a charity while you are alive.

Of the various techniques available, a *charitable remainder trust* is one to consider in many cases.

With a charitable remainder trust, you sign a trust agreement with an IRS approved charity and make a gift (e.g., stock) to the trust. You are actually only making a partial gift. The trust agreement says you are retaining, during your lifetime, income flowing from the gifted asset. The charity gets the asset (usually the remaining proceeds from the asset) only after you pass away.

Usually the gifted asset is one that has gone up in value since you purchased it. Once you set up the trust, the charity sells the asset instead of you. The charity pays no income tax on the gain (unlike what would happen if you sold the asset) because it is a tax-exempt entity. That means there is more to invest (because no income taxes are paid by the charity on any gain) and more to produce an income flow to you. The charity then invests all of the proceeds from the sale of the gift and pays you income for your lifetime in an amount based upon IRS regulations. When you pass away, the charity gets the remainder (that's why it's called a charitable remainder trust).

Assume you bought some stock for $50,000 and after many, many years it is now worth $250,000. If you sold the stock *without* using a charitable remainder trust, you would pay a capital gains income tax on the $200,000 profit (the $250,000 sales price less the $50,000 purchase price). So at a 28% capital gains tax rate the IRS would get about $56,000 of the proceeds leaving you with $194,000 to invest. With a charitable remainder trust, the full $250,000 would be available to invest on your behalf while you are alive.

By using a charitable remainder trust, you get an income tax deduction during your lifetime for the value of the gifted remainder to the charity and you are also reducing your estate for death tax purposes. Check with your accountant as to all of the tax ramifications and limitations and with your attorney as to the effect of such a trust on your qualifying for assistance with future nursing home care costs.

With a charitable remainder trust, you are giving up access to the gifted asset even if you need it for personal, medical, or other emergencies or for any reason. You will not be able to borrow on it or pass it on to your heirs or other loved ones. However, there are techniques such as a *life insurance trust* described in No. 55 on page 146 that may be available to make up for this "loss" to your heirs.

Since you are dealing with the long-term, you'll want to be affiliated with a charity that will be there as long as you are. You may be able to set up a charitable remainder trust with as little as $5,000 in cash or other acceptable asset worth that much or more.

With major charities, they may have the paperwork all ready to go. You may just need your legal advisor to review a short agreement and your tax/financial advisor to explain how this type of trust might work for you. However, have your attorney explain whether the terms of your trust would be subject to a special review and/or denial under a recent IRS ruling.

A special way "stay-at-home" parents can benefit by working part-time

Most baby boomer families have two parents working outside the home. As a result, both parents are earning coverage under Social Security for retirement benefits. What is often overlooked is that those parents are also earning benefits for themselves and their family if they become disabled or pass away. These benefits can be significant (see No. 2 on page 6 and the Appendix on pages 173 and 174).

A stay-at-home parent who works part-time (a home business is permissible, too) can also obtain Social Security benefits for himself or herself and the family. These benefits can be critical in helping the family if a tragedy strikes the stay-at-home parent.

To qualify for these benefits, enough *quarters of coverage* need to be earned (there are different eligibility rules for the various types of benefits). A quarter of coverage is earned by having wages or self-employment income at a high enough level for a given year (the dollar amount can change every year). In 1994, for example, earnings (or profits after expenses of your own business) needed to be at least $620 to receive one quarter of coverage. So, earnings (or business profits) of $2,480 in 1994 would have earned four quarters of coverage.

A stay-at-home parent working part-time might provide an extra safety net of Social Security benefits to pull the family through a tough time.

19.

Tickling your tickler: when to apply for Social Security and Medicare

Social Security says that baby boomers should retire at age 66 or 67 to get full benefits. Baby boomers born from 1946 to 1954 will be able to start taking full retirement benefits at age 66. For boomers born in 1955 or later, there will be an additional two-month waiting period for each succeeding year until you reach boomers who were born in 1960 or later, who will have to wait until reaching age 67 to attain "full retirement age."

When planning for your future, it would probably be a safe guess that Congress will eventually increase the full retirement age to age 70 for all baby boomers to help keep down the cost of baby boomer Social Security benefits.

Early, full and delayed retirement

You'll need to decide whether to take (1) early retirement age benefits, (2) full retirement benefits, or (3) delayed retirement benefits. As with all of life, there are trade-offs.

You need to look at your health status as well as your financial situation before deciding when to take Social Security retirement benefits.

You're not automatically paid Social Security benefits. You have to file a claim form and you should do so at least three months in advance of the desired starting date. You can contact your local Social Security office or call 1/800/772-1213 to find out how to file a claim.

If benefits are taken *early* (e.g., at age 63 for the first baby boomers), the benefits will be reduced by about 20%. So, for someone whose full retirement benefit would otherwise be $1,000 per month, it will be reduced down to $800 per month. However, the benefit would be received for several extra years by starting early at age 63. Also, if someone were not in good health, it might be very prudent to start benefits as early as possible. If you take early benefits on your working record and then want to claim higher benefits on your spouse's working record, be sure to contact Social Security again. Widows and widowers can take reduced benefits as early as age 50 in some cases.

If benefits are *delayed*, the benefits will increase by 8% per year for each year of delay. For example, if a full retirement benefit at age 66 were $1,000 per month and payments were delayed until age 71, the actual monthly benefit at age 71 would be $1,400 (8% per year times 5 years equals 40% and 40% of $1,000 equals $400 for a total benefit of $1,000 plus $400). With increased life spans, this might be a very attractive option.

Even if you delay taking Social Security benefits, don't forget to enroll for Medicare coverage three months prior to age 65 (or whatever age Congress later sets as a minimum for Medicare benefits). Although Medicare coverage is automatic when you apply for Social Security monthly benefits, it's not automatic if you're delaying the receipt of benefits and do not file any kind of application.

If you apply for Social Security retirement benefits, you are also automatically applying for certain Medicare coverage (Part A but not Part B) which will start at age 65. Basic (but inadequate) health coverage is given through Medicare Part A benefits. You will need extra health insurance through Medicare Part B coverage (which is obtained through Social Security) and/or through a Medigap policy (see page 111), which is issued by a private insurance company.

Other possible options to consider before attaining age 65 are joining a health maintenance organization (HMO) or getting a health insurance policy.

Hopefully, you won't be needy enough financially to qualify for *Medicaid*—a health care program for individuals with specified amounts of income and assets to establish eligibility.

And, as to health benefits, if you wait too long to apply, your private insurance could expire prior to activation of your Medicare coverage and you might be left without health insurance for a period of time.

Rules of programs will probably change over time. Perhaps the most important question to ask of any government program and private insurance policy under review is what is *not* covered.

Remember, the above guidelines deal with retirement benefits. Disability and survivors benefits may start far earlier.

Always contact Social Security at the earliest possible date to determine the eligibility of all possible family members for all possible benefits.

Too long a delay can mean a loss in benefits. You might discuss all of these matters with your parents, too.

Working and receiving benefits

If you work after starting to receive Social Security benefits, your wages are still subject to income tax and Social Security tax. Your wages may also reduce your Social Security benefits (depending upon your age and income). To know how much you are really netting from working, you must subtract income and employment taxes as well as any reductions in Social Security benefits.

Family benefits

For the boomers who will experience the simultaneous joy of retirement and having young children, don't overlook benefits that may also be payable to dependent children under age 18 or who are full time students between ages 18 and 22 or a child of any age if suffering from a disability that began before age 22. And, dependent parents may also receive benefits, too.

Income tax on Social Security benefits

Since you may owe income tax on Social Security benefits, depending upon your other income, you can reduce or avoid these taxes by controlling when you receive other income, including distributions from IRAs. You might also invest in Treasury bills or Series EE US Savings Bonds since the recognition of interest for income tax purposes might be pushed to a later year. You should talk to your tax advisor as to how different types of investments may affect your Social Security benefits.

MAKING THE KIDS AND STEP-KIDS WEALTHY AND WISE

20.

The right and wrong ways to save for your children's college education

Before you invest one penny for your children's college education, you need to determine whether investments should be made in your name or your children's. The consequences of this decision on your children qualifying for financial aid are enormous.

There are five basic sources for paying for your children's college education: (1) scholarships (including those in return for military service), (2) your children's earnings while going to school, (3) your children's savings, (4) your savings, and (5) financial aid. In most cases, it will take a combination of two or more of these sources to fund a college education.

The fifth source, financial aid, is very dependent upon the amount your children have saved and, to a much lesser degree, your level of savings, assets and income. Prior to opening up savings accounts and purchasing stocks, bonds and life insurance policies to fund a college education, you need to look at the long-term consequences of these actions.

Save in your name?

Should you save college money in your name or your children's? This decision will not just affect your children's ability to qualify for college education financial aid. It also has income tax, death tax and other implications.

Currently, colleges require students to spend much more of their money (over 33%) as compared to their parents' money (less than 10%) to pay for college education. This makes sense since students should pay to the extent they are capable of doing so. This approach will also make many parents set up a college savings fund in their names rather than their children's.

Another incentive to invest in your name is the income tax benefits with certain U.S. Savings Bonds. If these bonds are purchased in your name, used to pay for your children's college education and your income does not exceed certain limits, you can exclude the bond interest from your income for federal income tax purposes. Since this exclusion phases out as your income gets higher, you need to estimate your future income before deciding upon the actual benefit of this approach.

One danger of investing in your name, especially with blended families, is what can happen to the money if the blended family breaks up and a divorce occurs or if you pass away. Will half or more of the "college education fund" in your name that was intended for the education of your children from a former marriage be divided up with your current spouse?

Save in your children's names?

When parents put money or other assets in the names of their minor children to pay for future college expenses, they usually do it under the *Uniform Transfers to Minors Act (UTMA)* or the *Uniform Gifts to Minors Act (UGMA)*.

In general, with UTMA or UGMA, you can retain control as the manager (called the custodian) until the designated age (age 18 or sometimes age 21) is attained by a child of yours.

If you do not take certain steps when you set up the investments and you pass away before a child reaches the designated age, these assets that were "owned" by your children may be taxed in your estate for death tax purposes. You should consult with your attorney as to how to avoid that result.

Another risk of using UTMA or UGMA is that once a child reaches the designated age, the child is entitled to receive all of the assets in the account and use them in any manner. Your children may not want to use the funds to go to or stay in college.

Using trusts

Instead of putting assets in the name of your children, you might want to put some strings on the assets by creating one or more trusts for your children.

A trust could allow you to control the use of the funds.

Talk to your attorney about how such a trust could be written and the tradeoffs of this approach. Keep in mind that it will cost more now in attorney's fees to have trust provisions written as compared to setting up UTMA or UGMA accounts. Also, there will be greater legal and accounting costs through the years after your death in connection with such trusts for your children. Finally, the income tax laws on trusts keep changing and currently much more income tax is due on income that is kept in a trust rather than paid out to a trust beneficiary.

Kiddie Tax

Your family may not save income tax even if you try to shift some investments to your children to have them report the income on their tax return. *Kiddie Tax* says that until a child reaches age 14, a portion of the *unearned income* (e.g., interest and dividends as compared to wages from part-time work) may be taxed at the parents' federal income tax rate rather than the child's. This reduces the income tax incentive to shift income to your younger children. However, the first $1,200 of unearned income of a child under age 14 still receives preferential federal income tax treatment.

To put some perspective on the numbers, to earn $1,200 in one year with an 8% return, an investment of $15,000 would be required. Since it will take more than $15,000 to have a college fund, you need to consider the income tax implications of any college education fund, especially if any of your children are under the age of 14.

If unearned income exceeds the $1,200 per year amount, then the income tax strategies that make sense for a parent probably will also for your children (i.e., investing in income tax-free municipal bonds; delaying maturity dates of U.S. Series EE Bonds until after age 14 unless a child has already elected to report interest on bonds currently; and investing in mutual funds or stocks that pay little in the way of dividends and are held for long-term growth). This last technique, investing in stock mutual funds, has been very successful over the long haul since returns have averaged 10% per year on stocks. And, with stock mutual funds, since your child will probably be in a lower income tax bracket than you when the shares are sold, the tax bite at that time probably won't be as severe.

If your children are old enough to work in your family business, encourage them to help you out. Besides hopefully building a mutual appreciation for what each of you can do in the workplace, your children's earnings are not subject to the Kiddie Tax. Your children may even decide to open up IRAs with their earnings and be on the way to saving for retirement. However, an IRA has to be for the long haul (not for college) to avoid penalties and taxes on early withdrawals.

Other possible investments

There is a variety of other investments that may be appropriate for you in accumulating college education dollars.

Tuition prepayment plans. One possibility is to sign up for a tuition prepayment plan that guarantees the payments you make will cover tuition expenses regardless of future increases. What these plans do *not* guarantee is admission for your children to the institution of higher learning. Since you will be paying a fee through a reduced return to obtain this future cost protection, you need to compare the rate of return on this investment (and the institution's rules on withdrawals if you change your mind or your child does not want to go to college) with other forms of investing. Also, talk to your tax advisor as to whether these plans qualify for the *annual gift tax exclusion* (up to $10,000).

Life insurance policies. What about a life insurance policy on you that has a cash value building up inside it as a way to save for college? Since term life policies do not have a cash value build-up, you could consider using a non-term life insurance policy (probably a *variable cash value life insurance policy*) that invests in a mutual fund with growth stocks. It's risky, however, because if the investments do not work out, you can lose not only your cash value in the policy *but also* your coverage as well. On the other hand, if the investments do work out, you can reduce the size of your premium payments. The value inside such a policy would increase free of any income taxes. At college entrance time you could tap that cash value.

Instead of cashing in the policy to pay for college expenses, you could withdraw the cash value in a non-taxable policy loan to pay for college expenses. If you should die before your children were ready for college, the amount available would be even larger due to the life insurance component of the policy. And, yes, these death benefits could pass income-tax free to your children.

Usually it makes sense to use life insurance only if you need the insurance anyway and there are ten or more years until your children are applying for college since the surrender charges and fees may be too high compared with the return.

Steps to consider while a child is in high school

Usually two or three years in advance of college entrance time, you'll look into changing the form of any higher-risk investment (e.g., certain stocks and mutual funds) into a safer one producing a fixed rate of return (e.g., certificates of deposit).

One way to plan for the conversion of funds automatically is to purchase *zero-coupon municipal bonds*. With these bonds, you pay a discounted price now (e.g., $600) and when the bond matures, you receive the full price ($1,000). Your purchase of zero-coupon bonds can be staggered to mature one-fourth each year for four years. Of course, these days students are not usually graduating in just four years. You might want to build in a fifth year plan, too.

Another approach is to encourage your children to take advanced placement classes and tests to obtain college credit while in high school. This is one way to shorten the college tuition duration. Maybe you could offer your children a financial bonus if they get college credits in high school (e.g., give your children one-half of the savings for the earned units).

One final thought as tuition time rolls around involves grandparents. Although there is a federal gift tax exclusion for gifts of up to $10,000 per recipient per calendar year, there are two ways to make that amount unlimited. Certain payments of your children's unreimbursable, qualified medical expenses paid directly to the health care provider (medical insurance comes under this, too) are one way. The second way is for payments made directly to an educational institution for education expenses of another person. So imagine that—the wealthy grandpa or grandma can get a special break to reduce death taxes by paying their grandchildren's tuition, medical insurance and medical bills. There is some justice in the world after all.

21.

Calculating a college-size nest egg

The nest egg for a private university will probably need to be twice as large as one for a public university.

For a student entering college in 1994, the four-year total cost (tuition, books, room and board and other expenses) is around $40,000 for a public university and around $80,000 for a private university. As each year goes by, inflation will probably increase these costs at a 6% per year rate. That means an eight-year old will face public university costs of over $71,000 and private university costs of over $143,000.

These staggering costs point up the need to start saving now, so don't overlook the piggy bank saving technique to make the process easier (see No. 1 on page 5). The good news is that you can cut in half the amount you need to save if your children go to a public university.

Should you plan to save all of the costs?

It may be unrealistic for you to assume you can save 100% of these probable college costs. Whatever you can save will be a big help. If you can manage to save one-half or two-thirds of the needed amount, you will have achieved a great deal. Any savings you already have in place for college costs will also reduce the monthly amount needed to accumulate the desired college nest egg.

Your children may be able to pay for the difference through loans, scholarships or other financial aid, including work-study programs. As last resorts to be avoided if possible, you might tap into the equity in your home or a retirement plan to raise necessary funds.

The effect of inflation on college costs

The table below shows how 6% per year inflation will drive up private and public college education costs.

Your child's year of birth	Total 4-year cost at private university	Total 4-year cost at public university
1976	$ 80,000	$ 40,000
1977	84,800	42,400
1978	89,888	44,944
1979	95,281	47,641
1980	100,998	50,499
1981	107,058	53,529
1982	113,482	56,741
1983	120,290	60,145
1984	127,508	63,754
1985	135,158	67,579
1986	143,268	71,634
1987	151,863	75,932
1988	160,976	80,488
1989	170,634	85,317
1990	180,872	90,436
1991	191,725	95,862
1992	203,228	101,614
1993	215,422	107,711
1994	228,347	114,174
1995	242,048	121,024
1996	256,571	128,285
1997	271,965	135,983
1998	288,283	144,141
1999	305,580	152,790

The next table shows how much you would need to save each month to reach your goal. The first monthly savings column shows the amount of monthly savings you'd need to reach 50% of the expected public university cost. The second monthly savings column shows both the amount of monthly savings for 50% of the private university cost or 100% of the public university cost—they are the same amount since it costs about twice as much for a private university.

Your child's year of birth	Monthly savings for 50% of public university cost	Monthly savings for 50% of private university cost or 100% of public university cost
1977	$1,699	$3,397
1978	866	1,731
1979	588	1,176
1980	449	898
1981	366	732
1982	310	620
1983	271	542
1984	241	481
1985	217	434
1986	199	398
1987	183	366
1988	170	341
1989	159	318
1990	150	299
1991	142	283
1992	134	268
1993	128	256
1994	122	244
1995	117	234
1996	124	248
1997	131	262
1998	139	278
1999	148	295

The last table was based on starting to save for college costs from scratch on January 1, 1995, earning 8% per year (before taxes) on the investments and reinvesting all the earnings. However, if your child was born in 1996 or later, then the table assumes you started to save on January 1 of the year in which your child was born.

The earlier you start, the smaller your monthly nut

What the last table on page 67 shows is the benefit of starting to save early. If your goal is to save 50% of the cost of a four-year education in a public university, you can achieve that goal under the stated assumptions by saving $117 per month if a child is born in 1995 and you start saving right away.

If you delay saving for that same child until your child is three years away from entering college, you need to put away more than $2,900 *per month* (that calculation is not in the table).

To meet your savings goal, you should try to set up an arrangement whereby funds are withdrawn automatically from your checking account and put into your college fund investments.

Each year, you should review with your financial advisor both the rate of return on your investments and the college cost inflation rate to see that you are staying on schedule in your savings program.

22.

Paying your children to learn and saving money at the same time

Don't overlook a great way to save money—paying your growing children to learn the value of a dollar.

Every dollar you don't spend on the latest toy or fad can be invested for your children's future. You can make your children part of the financial team, teaching them the value of a dollar and math skills as well.

Want to teach your children subtraction? Go to the market with your children and say the following: "Here are the names of two brands of cleanser and each one is 16 ounces. If you pick the less expensive one, you can keep the difference in cost (or use that money to buy a special treat) if you can calculate the amount in your head."

You might want to teach addition by giving them grocery coupons, having them find the coupon items and again, using their head and not a calculator, come up with the right total to pocket the coupon savings. This might even be a way to get the kids to do most of the legwork while shopping.

Since you can't get kids to save easily, you might involve their division skills by letting them spend (within certain guidelines) one-half of these savings and saving the balance. You'd be amazed how quickly children can learn to divide by two or multiply by 50 percent when the correct answers mean money in hand.

Once these skills have been mastered, you can work on multiplication by using the same approach that gives you an incentive to save at work. Retirement plans such as a 401(k) plan often offer matching contributions by employers. Why not start your own matching savings plan for your children? If they save, you'll match it in part or in whole.

You could match a portion of their contributions to a savings or mutual fund account. For example, you could put in 20% of your children's contribution for the first $100 in savings to make the total $120. Then, once another plateau was reached such as $500, you could increase your contribution rate for new savings to 30% so that the next $100 saved by your children would be matched by a 30% contribution ($30) by you.

You could give a bigger allowance according to the amount of the chores done. This might relieve you of too heavy a workload at home, teach your children the value of work and money and give your children a sense of accomplishment. Why not try it?

You could even teach compound interest by playing "what if" games with your children? You could say to a nine-year-old, if you put $100 in a savings account or mutual funds and it grows every year at 8% per year, how much will *you* have at age 12? 15? 18? They might get very interested in calculating their future net worth.

Pretty soon your kids will want to know about the "rule of 72"—you know, the one that says, you can calculate how many years it will take to double your money by dividing 72 by the rate of return (e.g., 72 divided by 8, for 8%, will take 9 years to double your money).

By the way, when the nine-year old (two paragraphs back) attains age 18, that $100 will have doubled to $200 without any other contributions having been made.

23.

Keeping Uncle Sam out of your estate

You can take steps to reduce or eliminate federal death tax and have more on hand for your children. Death tax starts at 37% and goes up from there.

On what size estate is federal death tax due?

For most people, the magic number is $600,000 as to whether there will be any federal death tax. For estates below that size, no federal death tax should be due.

You should pay attention as to how that $600,000 amount is determined. First, add up *all* your assets such as real estate, cash, stocks, bonds, business interests, cars, and personal items. Then, add up your IRAs, retirement plans, and certain life insurance policies (the ones controlled by you) and all of your other assets. Next, subtract your debts and liabilities (such as mortgages, car loans, and personal loans). If the remainder is below $600,000, then, in general, there won't be any federal death tax. However, it's quite possible that this $600,000 exemption amount will be lowered to $200,000 or $300,000 to help pay for national health reform and/or reduce the national debt.

Married couples can exempt up to $1,200,000

Depending upon how a husband and wife set up their wills, trusts and ownership of assets, they could each potentially have a $600,000 exemption or a total $1.2 million exemption for the family.

Let's look at how this could work for a couple worth $600,000 each for a total of $1.2 million together. This number is not far-fetched for many couples when you realize that life insurance (unless special steps are taken in advance—see below) and retirement plan benefits are part of the equation.

$235,000 in unnecessary death tax

If one spouse worth $600,000 leaves all of his or her assets outright to the surviving spouse, then the survivor will be worth $1.2 million at the time of his or her death. If the surviving spouse can only shield $600,000 from death tax, then the remaining $600,000 will be taxed. The federal death tax in this scenario would be $235,000. There is a way to keep that $235,000 within the family instead of making this donation to the IRS.

Death tax savings trust

This $235,000 federal death tax could go down to zero on the $1.2 million in assets if the first spouse to die had set up a will or trust with a *death tax saving trust* (sometimes called a *B trust, credit shelter trust* or *exemption trust*). The reason is that assets of the first to die in a properly drafted death tax saving trust will not be counted as being owned by the surviving spouse. The assets of the first to die would be shielded from death tax by the $600,000 exemption permitted for the first to die.

With a death tax saving trust in a will or trust, the surviving spouse could be the beneficiary of the trust and, in some cases, be the trustee (manager) of the trust as well. Your attorney can explain how this type of trust works.

Ask your attorney if there will be state inheritance tax and/or federal and state income tax even if there is no federal death tax.

Ways to increase the $600,000 exemption

If you pass away leaving a surviving spouse and an estate larger than $600,000, there are ways to leave the excess above $600,000 to your spouse with no federal death tax due at your death. If your will or trust qualifies for the federal *marital deduction*, there may be no federal death tax due at the time the first spouse dies.

Keep in mind that if the assets you are leaving to your spouse qualify for this marital deduction, there may only be a delay, or deferral, of death tax until your spouse dies. The assets that qualify for the marital deduction (or what's left of them) are then counted in the survivor's taxable estate. This will increase the size of the survivor's estate. For details on the marital deduction, contact your estate planning attorney.

Another way to exempt more than the $600,000 amount is by making gifts during your lifetime. Only certain kinds of gifts, however, qualify to stretch the exempt amount. So, review any proposed gift with your attorney before making the gift to determine whether it eats into your $600,000 exemption instead of stretching it.

In general, you can make lifetime gifts of up to $10,000 per calendar year per recipient that do not use up any part of your $600,000 exemption. Husbands and wives can usually double these $10,000 amounts if certain technical requirements are met. You can also stretch the $10,000 amount by paying tuition and/or medical expenses directly to providers on be-half of the persons you want to benefit.

It's important to understand the consequences of lifetime gifts before the gifts are made. Some gifts may increase the overall tax to your family. With advance planning, you can some-times restructure a gift so that it produces a tax benefit you would otherwise have lost. Since states have their own rules on these matters, you cannot ignore state law consequences.

Besides lifetime gifts, another way is to shift an "opportunity" (e.g., an investment) to your children well in advance of your death where there is a good likelihood that the opportunity will grow in value.

Also, certain family partnership arrangements and/or lifetime transfers of interests in family businesses or property, including the use of trusts, can reduce the tax bite.

You should review this area very carefully with your estate planning attorney since there are special rules for family transactions.

Finally, consider taking steps regarding life insurance to alter the common result of life insurance being subject to death tax. There are special ways to own life insurance so you can pass on large amounts of life insurance to your children without any death tax due on the proceeds (See No. 55 on page 146). Consult with your attorney on the ways to achieve this result.

TYING OR RETYING
THE KNOT

24.

What you must know before you marry or remarry

Whether you are planning to marry for the first time or get remarried, you need to do some advance planning to avoid some surprises down the road.

You'll want to consider how title (ownership) is taken on assets each of you own now and may own in the future, such as bank accounts and a house, so that the intended beneficiaries inherit upon a death.

For example, if you own assets with your spouse as joint tenants, your children from a former marriage may get nothing upon your death even if your will leaves everything to them. Why? Because, in general, certain ways of holding title (ownership) such as joint tenancy *override* a will or trust.

How you take title may also impact how assets will be divided in case this marriage (or remarriage) doesn't work out.

Title to assets can also affect income taxes for the surviving spouse and death taxes for the family.

You should sign a new will and/or trust after getting married. If you don't do so, the law will probably assume that you wanted to carve out a sizeable share or all of your estate for your spouse but just never got around to doing so.

You need to think through the provisions of a new will or trust. You might say, "I want to leave everything to my kids from my former marriage." What if your spouse sold his or her residence to move into your house? You may want to provide for your surviving spouse. Would you want your spouse to have to move out right after your death or would you instead allow your spouse some time to live there and plan the next move? Would your spouse be paying rent or taking care of expenses on the residence during that time period? What about the furnishings in the residence? If they had belonged to you, would you want your spouse left without a stick of furniture? Take a look at No. 30 on pages 87 and 88 for additional suggestions in providing for a surviving spouse and protecting your children from a former marriage.

If you have young children, you'll need to think about who should be named as the guardian to raise them.

See No. 27 on page 83 to see how your marriage could affect college financial aid.

All of these issues need to be coordinated in a master plan worked out with your attorney so that no element is working at cross purposes with the rest of the plan. You should re-view with your attorney, before the marriage, your potential liability for debts of your spouse, including tax obligations.

Before you go to the altar, go to your attorney to discuss the reasons for considering a marital agreement.

Finally, take a look at No. 43 on pages 119 to 120, which discusses considerations for your parents' remarrying because these issues may apply to you, too.

25.

Will Uncle Sam tear up part of your marital agreement?

Assume many years ago you signed a beneficiary designation naming your two grown children from a prior marriage as the beneficiaries on your long-standing retirement plan. Let's say you remarry, and a marital agreement is signed saying what's yours is yours and what's mine is mine, including retirement plan assets. After the remarriage, you sign a new will leaving everything to your children. If this new marriage lasts two years and then you pass away, who will get the retirement assets?

It may be that your surviving spouse will receive all of the benefits through an annuity that lasts for the spouse's lifetime. Why? Depending upon the type of retirement plan, federal law may say that your spouse must be the sole beneficiary because your spouse never signed a necessary *waiver* form after the marriage concerning retirement plan benefits.

This can distort your intended result, especially if the retirement plan is a major asset in the estate. Talk to your attorney about the steps you can take to avoid this confusion.

26.

Saving a fortune by delaying the wedding day

Imagine sometime in the future you are getting married or remarried. You and your future spouse each own a house. At least one of the two houses will be sold in the near future and the other one may be sold soon or down the road. To understand why you *may* want to sell one or both houses before you get married, read on.

You bought your house for $75,000 and you're ready to sell it for $200,000. You could pay *no income tax* on the sale if you qualified for a special exclusion described below. Many state laws are similar.

Your spouse-to-be is in a similar situation having purchased a house for $100,000 that is now worth $225,000. Your future spouse could pay *no income tax* on the sale if the timing were right.

Special exclusion from income tax

Up to $125,000 of gain on the sale of a residence can be eliminated by individuals who qualify for a special income tax *once-in-a-lifetime exclusion*.

Who gets the exclusion? There are several requirements. First, you need to be at least age 55 (so be thinking about your parents for now and yourself for the future). Second, you must have owned and used the residence as your principal residence for a total of at least three years during the five-year period ending on the date of sale. Third, you need to make a *special election* on a form that is attached to your income tax return.

Since this is a once-in-a-lifetime exclusion, you want to pick the right spot at the right time to use it. You don't need to reinvest the proceeds of the sale of one residence into another residence to get this tax benefit.

It's all in the timing

So, what's the catch? If you wait to sell either or both houses *until after* the marriage, as a married couple you only get one $125,000 exclusion, not two.

If, instead, each of you met the requirements and completed the sale of your houses *before* your wedding date, you could each exclude $125,000 in gain.

If one of you had used the exclusion before you married each other, neither of you could use it again after you married. This would be an incentive for the spouse who hadn't used the exclusion to sell his or her house *before* the wedding date and use his or her exclusion.

Also, if you make such an election during your marriage and later divorce, no further election is available to either of you or your future spouses should either of you remarry.

Ask your tax advisor and attorney about all the details and (1) how to reduce the three-year requirement if someone has been incapacitated, hospitalized, or in a nursing home; (2) how temporary or seasonal absences may be counted towards the required time period; (3) how the $125,000 amount is reduced if you are a married person filing a separate income tax return; and (4) how an unmarried widow or widower may be able to use his or her $125,000 exclusion if the deceased spouse already used the exemption before the marriage.

Remember, this is a one-time exclusion. Save it for the biggest gain you'll ever have. If you have a $20,000 gain and use the exclusion, you won't be able to use the exclusion again for the balance of the $125,000 maximum amount.

27.

Filling out college aid applications before and after the wedding

Becoming a step-parent can have quite an impact on a child's or step-child's chance of qualifying for college aid programs.

If you're a single parent, you are not reporting the income and assets of anyone except yourself.

Once you get married (or remarried), you are then part of a team and the financial situation of the entire team needs to be considered.

Federal aid programs consider the income of the custodial parents. If you are not yet married, then your children are not reporting the income of your spouse-to-be. When you and your spouse say "I do," each of you may be saying "I'll pay" for the college education of your step-children when they have a second custodial parent.

That means the financial picture of both parents enters into the equation to determine *eligibility* for college aid, even if you've signed a pre-marital agreement saying each of you will pay for your own children's education. Ask your attorney whether your state law requires a different arrangement.

28.

For better or for worse—what can that *really* mean?

Before you tie the knot, check to see whether Social Security benefits will be affected by your marriage. For example, a divorced person claiming benefits on an ex-spouse's working record could lose those benefits by remarrying.

You also should get advice on your potential liability as a spouse and on ways to protect your assets.

You need to know the implications of putting your new spouse on title to the residence you brought into the marriage. Will the house be sold if your spouse's business venture goes belly up? Will the house be sold due to a debt incurred before the marriage that was never paid off? How will the house be divided if the marriage breaks up?

Finally, will the government force you to use your assets to pay for your spouse's nursing home costs and medical bills even if you've signed a marital agreement saying you'll each pay your own way?

Buy some time for a consultation with an attorney so you can ease your concerns and enjoy your marriage.

29.

The surprise death tax: how surviving spouses may avoid paying unnecessary death taxes

If your spouse dies, you may think that there's no federal death tax on what you inherit from your spouse. You could be right and you could be wrong. It depends.

There are two main ways a surviving spouse could be surprised with a death tax.

One: Retirement plan distributions

Retirement plan distributions could be subject to death tax upon the death of a spouse depending upon (1) the size of the estate; (2) the form of retirement plan distributions (*lump sum* as compared to *annuity payouts*); (3) who is the beneficiary; and (4) how a will or trust reads.

In general, there are ways to avoid death tax on the death of the first spouse no matter the size of an estate (including estates larger than $600,000). The key is to coordinate your will and/or trust and beneficiary designations to take advantage of the death tax benefits available.

What has become tricky is whether retirement plan payouts (including those from company plans, Keogh plans and IRAs) qualify for this special tax break. This is something to look into while you and your spouse are both alive so the surviving spouse does not have to pay unnecessary death tax after the death of the first spouse. If you don't plan in advance, the survivor and/or the children may be left with much less than planned. Since you can take steps to prevent a problem, consult with your attorney to obtain the desired result.

Two: Spouses who are not U.S. citizens

If you are married and you and/or your spouse are permanent resident(s) but not U.S. citizens, you *may* need to obtain legal assistance to avoid death tax on the first death. You and your spouse may want to set up a will or trust that includes a *QDOT*.

QDOT stands for "qualified domestic trust" and it is a special trust that allows a non-citizen surviving spouse to delay paying death tax upon the first spouse's death. The death tax, however, may be paid during the survivor's lifetime or at the survivor's death, depending upon the assets in the trust and the timing of distributions from the trust. If this sounds complicated, it is. That's why you need an attorney to guide you through this legal jungle. However, not every estate will require such a trust.

30.

Protecting the inheritance for your kids

If you are in your first marriage or a remarriage, there is a way you can benefit your spouse under your will or trust but also make sure your children are the beneficiaries of what's left over after your spouse passes away.

This technique is called a QTIP (*qualified terminable interest property*) trust. This type of trust gives you some control over assets left to benefit your spouse. It allows your spouse to benefit from your assets but at the same time gives you the final say as to the ultimate beneficiaries once your surviving spouse passes away (even if your spouse remarries).

The best planning in a will or trust will all go out the window unless you hold title (ownership) to your assets in a way that complements your intended plan. Otherwise, assets may pass outside the will or trust to unintended beneficiaries.

You'll also need to review with your attorney how beneficiary designations on life insurance, IRA, 401(k), and other retirement plans should read after a marriage. You may need to have your spouse sign a special waiver so certain retirement benefits go to someone other than your spouse (e.g., your children from a prior marriage).

If you are remarrying and you and/or your future spouse have children from a former marriage, talk to your attorney about how your will or trust may benefit or exclude step-children. If you don't deal with this issue, it may be that upon your death your state law will give step-children and your children equal shares of your estate. This is fine if it's what you want to happen. But do your family a favor and don't have everyone guessing and paying attorney's fees to sort things out after your death.

Finally, be sure that your will and/or trust says who will pay death taxes. Otherwise, it could be that your spouse or a child receives an asset outside the will or trust but only the beneficiaries under the will or trust pay the death taxes on that asset. This could result in a total depletion of assets passing under the will or trust.

Instead, it may be preferable that each beneficiary, whether inheriting under your will or trust or receiving an asset through a beneficiary designation, pay his or her fair share of death tax according to how much was received.

MORE WAYS
TO PROTECT
THE NEST EGG

31.

Refinancing for the better

The biggest expense for most baby boomers is their home mortgage. One great way to cut down costs and provide extra funds for retirement and education planning may be to refinance the home mortgage when rates are advantageous.

Be aware, however, if you refinance, there may be a prepayment penalty (see No. 12 on page 36) and not all of the interest may be deductible (check with your accountant). Also see No. 40 on page 106.

There is also one hidden aspect of refinancing that may affect your nest egg in an unexpected way.

When you buy a house and take out a loan as part of the purchase, some states give you special protection in that you may have no *personal liability* if you do not complete the payments on the mortgage. The lender in those cases may only go against the house and not your other assets to collect on the house loan.

When you refinance, you are probably giving up that protection because the refinanced loan was not taken out at the time of purchase. There may be circumstances where this personal liability potential could affect your decision to refinance. You should obtain appropriate assistance on this matter.

32.

Protecting retirement plan assets

There are four main ways you can protect retirement plan assets. Three of the techniques protect you and one protects your heirs.

First, be diligent concerning the investment of retirement plan assets. More and more you'll see fraudulent, pie-in-the-sky schemes to lure retirement investors.

Second, become aware of the tax rules on different types of distributions (such as *lump sum* vs. *annuity payouts*), how extra *excise taxes* may reduce the available retirement plan proceeds while you are alive or after you are gone, and how beneficiary designations can affect the deferral of income tax. Also, by retirement age, you should become aware of how distributions could increase the income tax on your Social Security benefits.

Third, if you own a business, be aware that different types of retirement plans offer different degrees of protection in case you ever need to file bankruptcy. With some types of plans, you may be able to keep the retirement plan assets from going to creditors as part of a bankruptcy. With other types of plans, the retirement plan assets could be totally lost. You should talk to your attorney about the possibilities for your situation.

Fourth, ask your attorney how to complete beneficiary designations to prevent retirement plan assets from going through *probate* unnecessarily if you die. Probate would result in higher attorney's fees and assets possibly going to creditors instead of your family (see No. 35 on page 95).

33.

Life insurance do's and don'ts

Although state laws generally protect life insurance proceeds from creditors, there is one way that the proceeds can get thrown in the pot and be subject to the claims of creditors: if one's estate is named as the beneficiary on a life insurance policy, then the proceeds may not only have to go through probate unnecessarily but they also can be claimed by creditors, justly or unjustly.

Life insurance may also end up in your probate estate if all of the beneficiaries you name on the designation form fail to survive you. If you named your parents as the primary and backup beneficiaries on a policy and they both pass away before you, the life insurance proceeds would probably end up in your probate estate. Instead, if you had updated your beneficiary designations, the proceeds could have been paid quickly and correctly to the beneficiaries you had in mind without having to go through probate. (See No. 35 on page 95 for a further discussion of probate).

So, talk to your attorney about how to fill out your beneficiary designations forms. The forms may look insignificant but the choice of a few words can affect generations.

Also, don't assume that life insurance will escape death tax. You need to take special steps as described in No. 55 on page 146.

34.

How to plan for rainy days: umbrella insurance

This is not a society where people are shy about suing.

The usual amount of car insurance doesn't protect you against the major losses that can easily occur.

One relatively inexpensive solution is to have *umbrella insurance* on top of your regular car and home liability insurance. This kind of insurance starts paying when your other insurance coverage is exhausted. You may be able to get up to $1 million, $2 million or more of coverage for far less than you think.

Ask your liability insurance agent about umbrella insurance. That way you may not get soaked when a bit of rain pours into your life.

35.

Avoiding probate with a living trust

Usually when you pass away your estate will go through *probate*. Probate is the legal procedure set up by your state to see that taxes, debts, and expenses are paid and your remaining assets are distributed to the correct beneficiaries or heirs. This procedure is supervised by a court sometimes referred to as the "probate court." Most people associate probate with high attorney and executor fees, delays, and hassles.

One way to avoid probate is to set up and transfer your assets to a *living trust*. A living trust is a legal document spelling out the management and distribution of your assets while you are alive *and* after you die. The main difference between a will and a living trust is that upon a death a living trust may avoid the probate court altogether.

In general, setting up a living trust provides no protection against creditors. Since you can revoke the trust and maintain total control over your assets, you are still considered the owner of the assets while you are alive. At your death, the assets in the trust are usually subject to claims by your creditors.

One way that may provide additional protection against creditors is holding title in *joint tenancy*. State law will determine if that's the case. Ask your attorney about the tax and non-tax ramifications on holding title in joint tenancy (see also pages 125 to 127).

36.

Family limited partnerships:
keeping it all in the family

One estate planning technique for combining death tax planning and potential creditor protection is a *family limited partnership*.

This arrangement calls for you and your children to sign a limited partnership agreement. You put certain assets into the partnership and in return you receive partnership interests. You can control the partnership as the managing partner. You can then give some of these partnership interests to your children each year as a gift.

This technique can reduce death taxes by reducing the size of your estate. Each gift of the partnership interests to your children reduces your estate. And, concerning the partnership interests you still own at death, your estate may be entitled to a discount in their value because what you own is no longer 100 percent of the partnership. The result may be a much lower death tax for the family to pay.

As a side benefit, you may have some creditor protection because it will usually be more difficult for a creditor to go after a limited partnership interest and see money in hand. The law in this area is evolving, however, and the trend will probably be to help creditors.

Very often the family limited partnership is combined with using a corporation and an *irrevocable trust*; however, there are considerable attorney, accountant, and appraisal fees, so this technique may not be for everyone.

37.

Irrevocable trusts: do's and don'ts

Irrevocable trusts are most often used for reducing death tax (through gifts or as a way to own life insurance) or setting up an education fund. In general, they cannot be changed after they are established. Due to the finality and legal cost of these documents, you should enter into them cautiously.

If you are truly giving assets away, be absolutely sure you will never need those assets again. Although you may trust your child completely, you may be unprotected if your child dies or becomes disabled and no provision has been set up for your possible benefit.

Irrevocable life insurance trusts are a way to purchase life insurance and keep Uncle Sam from becoming a co-beneficiary of the proceeds.

Grantor retained income trusts (GRITS) are irrevocable trusts that leverage your $600,000 exemption (see No. 23 on pages 71 through 74) from death tax. These trusts allow you to keep the income for a number of years from an asset put in the trust and then transfer the asset to the beneficiaries during your lifetime. The result can be a dramatic reduction in death tax.

Remember, however, there may be income tax disadvantages in making lifetime gifts through irrevocable trusts. In some cases, it would be a better tax result for the beneficiaries to have received or inherited the asset upon your death. It all depends upon the nature of the asset, the potential for growth in value of the asset, the purchase price or tax basis of the asset, and the size of your estate.

Some irrevocable trusts may provide protection against creditors.

In summary, irrevocable trusts are not for everyone. Usually, the greater your wealth, the greater the possible need for this technique. Check with your attorney.

MOVING TO
GREENER PASTURES

38.

Finding the right place for your parents to retire

As a baby boomer, there's a good chance you'll need to help take care of your parents.

Physical proximity to your parents can be of great comfort to them and to you. It can also help you avoid disruptions at work, which is important in these days of job insecurity.

When our parents need us, there's usually a crisis that may linger on for years. With blended families, we may be stretched out literally and figuratively as parents, step-parents, siblings, and step-siblings relocate across the country.

By the year 2004, baby boomers will range in age from 40 to 58. Our parents will be in their 60s, 70s, 80s or 90s, and many of them will need personal care and help from their baby boomer children. Where your parents, step-parents, and other close relatives will be living in relation to you will be important.

There are financial implications relating to where one lives. For example, different states have different rules for determining eligibility for governmental assistance in paying for nursing home costs. Don't assume that because you have become educated about the rules in one state (and that your parents would qualify in that state) that your parents will qualify if they move to another state. This is an important item to be checked out with an attorney before any final decisions are made by your parents.

Qualifying for eligibility can be tricky in two circumstances. First, if your parents live in one state part of the year and in another state the rest of the year, both states could say that your parents need to apply for assistance in the *other* state.

Second, a problem could occur if your parents first move from their home state to another state for retirement, then later return to the original home state and an illness occurs. The home state may try to claim that the true permanent residence is not there, but is instead in the retirement state.

These possibilities point up the good sense of obtaining legal advice on how to sever ties with a state (e.g., voting in the new state, getting a driver's license in the new state, signing a will or trust in the new state, etc.) and whether it is advisable to do so.

The ability to pay long-term nursing home costs can thus be affected by where your parents live. For more information, refer to No. 41 and No. 42 on pages 109 to 116.

Your parents will also face the issues described in No. 39 on pages 103 through 105.

39.

Five questions you need to ask before moving to a new state or staying right where you are

Most of us assume we can live anywhere in the United States and the laws and rules will be pretty much the same. As discussed in No. 38, the implementation of the rules on governmental assistance for nursing home costs differ from state to state.

There are five questions you need to ask before making a move. Your parents need to get the answers to these questions, too, before they start packing their bags.

1. Will my marital agreement be enforceable in the new state?

A marital agreement valid in one state may not be enforceable if you move to another state. Also, the rules for the necessary elements in the agreement may be different, depending upon whether the agreement was signed before or after the marriage. You might need to sign another agreement in the new state if your spouse is agreeable.

2. Will my will or trust work the same in the new state?

The laws for wills, trusts and inheritance are not identical in every state. Everyone who moves to a new state should have his or her will or trust reviewed by an attorney in the new state to be sure no surprises arise down the line. For example, in these days of blended families, it's important to ask an attorney in the new state what the rights, if any, would be for step-children if you did not revise your will or trust.

3. Are the income tax laws different in the new state and will I still be subject to income tax in the old state after I move?

There are different state income tax laws across the country. As you look for a place to retire or decide to buy a house now for the retirement years, you might seek out a state without an income tax. If you earn a pension in a state with an income tax and then move to a state with no income tax, you might find the income tax authorities of the first state trying to follow the pension income to the new state to tax it. Their rationale is that you earned the pension while you were living in the old home state so they should have the right to tax it no matter where you are living in retirement. You should check with your accountant on this issue (also see question 5 on the next page).

4. Are the property tax laws different in the new state?

Property tax laws differ across the country. Some states give special property tax breaks to senior citizens. Others allow children to receive special tax benefits if they inherit or receive real estate as a gift.

One state, for example, might allow property taxes to avoid an increase after your death only to the extent your children, and not your grandchildren, inherit real estate from you. With this in mind, you might change your will or trust to allocate your house only to your children and have other assets go to your grandchildren to take advantage of this property tax benefit.

5. Are the inheritance tax laws the same in both states?

Talk to your legal and financial advisor about whether the inheritance tax laws are more favorable in one state as compared to another and whether you should take certain steps (e.g., voting in the new state, getting a driver's license in the new state, signing a will or trust in the new state, etc.) to establish a *domicile* (i.e., permanent residence) to determine where you should be taxed. Also, find out if you can avoid having a probate upon your death in any state, let alone in more than one state.

If you split your time between two or more states, both states may try to take a tax bite out of your estate at your death. Or, one state may have no inheritance tax and the other state may have a steep tax and you can guess which one would like to go after a piece of your estate.

40.

Paying all cash for your home
for retirement may not be wise

When you start thinking of buying your dream home to live out the retirement years, you might want to avoid making an all-cash purchase (even if this luxury is possible).

First, you'll be tying up a large portion of your assets in an illiquid (hard-to-sell) asset by paying all cash.

Second, if you borrow against the property in the future after the purchase is completed, there may be personal liability on the loan you could have avoided by taking out the loan at the time of purchase (see No. 31 on page 91).

Finally, you may not be able to deduct all the interest on a loan taken out after the purchase of a property. Ask your accountant about limitations on deducting interest.

NURSING HOME NEWS

41.

What your parents should be doing now to avoid going broke paying future nursing home costs

Planning your retirement should consider the future needs of your parents, which could affect you emotionally as well as financially. One of their greatest needs may be paying for nursing home costs. Probably about half of the parents of baby boomers will need nursing home care.

Nursing home costs can range from $1,500 to $8,000 per month. The costs may be doubled if both parents require this care.

How do the elderly pay for nursing costs now? Some pay their own way and others qualify for governmental assistance through Medicare or Medicaid. Medicare pays for a very small portion of the country's long-term nursing home costs since it has limited skilled nursing home care benefits. More extensive nursing home coverage is available through Medicaid but this program is only for individuals who have established financial need. Your parents should check with their attorney to learn how ownership of a house is treated under this program.

Paying their own way

No. 42 (on pages 115 and 116) discusses a new long-term care insurance program that can protect assets for residents of some states; however, even if this new insurance will be available to or affordable by your parents, other ways to pay these costs should be reviewed.

Many parents of baby boomers are house rich and cash poor. How will they pay their own way for nursing home or other long-term care?

One option is to mine the value out of the family residence. It may be feasible for you or someone else to buy your parents' house and lease it back to them. Then, the purchase payments could pay for the needed care. Before taking this step, your parents should obtain legal and tax advice.

Another possibility is for your parents to take out a loan against their house. One potential problem with this approach is how the loan will be repaid.

A solution might be to have a loan known as a *reverse mortgage*. A reverse mortgage has the lending company paying the homeowner a certain amount each month (for *possibly* as long as the homeowner is alive) rather than the homeowner paying the lender each month (that's why it's called a reverse mortgage).

A reverse mortgage is very often used to provide additional income during retirement. With this type of loan, the homeowner is gambling that he or she will live long enough for the benefits of the monthly payments to outweigh the costs of the loan.

When is a reverse mortgage repaid? A reverse mortgage may require repayment when the homeowner dies, sells the house or enters a nursing home. If this third condition is part of the loan requirements, then this type of loan will not work to help pay for nursing home care.

A reverse mortgage needs to be reviewed carefully in advance by an attorney and qualified tax advisor because (1) it may give the lender the right to sell the house at a moment that is not beneficial for the family (e.g., when your parent enters the nursing home, the real estate market may be low) but is sufficient to pay the lender back, and (2) there is often a guaranteed fee for the lender (which is really additional interest) that could amount to hundreds of thousands of dollars even if the payments to your parents only last a short period of time.

Medigap insurance is not enough

Since Medicare does not cover all health expenses, there is usually a need for a supplemental health insurance policy commonly called a *Medigap* policy.

Although the name implies this type of policy is designed to fill in the gaps of Medicare coverage, there will probably still be a need for yet another policy to cover long-term care (including nursing home) costs. With health reform about to change the landscape, you'll need to keep up to date with developments concerning the coverage provided by various types of policies.

Long-term care insurance

In addition to a Medigap policy, your parents probably should have a *long-term care insurance policy*. Before your parents sign an application for such a policy, they should review with their attorney (1) the need for such a policy, (2) what alternatives are available, and (3) the terms and conditions of the policy.

Actually, you don't need to be elderly to buy and benefit from long-term care insurance. Younger people can use this coverage, too, if they suffer from heart attacks, strokes, cancer or even automobile accidents.

Age and health conditions may mean that your parents will not be eligible for this insurance. If your parents are eligible, see how their proposed (or current) policy covers the following items:

1. Alzheimer's disease should definitely be covered under the policy as well as Parkinson's disease. Check to see if any illnesses are not covered.

2. Pre-existing conditions should be covered (there will probably be a waiting period for such conditions—make sure the waiting period does not start anew each time a parent gets treated for the condition—otherwise the benefits may never be payable).

3. The policy benefits should be payable without having to first be hospitalized or in a skilled nursing facility before the nursing home stay begins.

4. The policy should be guaranteed renewable so it cannot be cancelled by the insurance company.

5. The premiums should be guaranteed to avoid increases if your parents' health worsens or as they get older (see if premiums are returned if your parents don't need the insurance benefits).

6. Review the maximum benefits during their lifetime as well as how they are calculated—per illness, per stay, a maximum dollar amount, a maximum number of days (look at competitive policies to get the best coverage).

7. Make sure the benefits can't be reduced.

8. Try to have an inflation protection option to increase the amount of benefits.

9. Check to see if your parents must live in a certain geographic area to receive the benefits under the policy in case your parents need to move (e.g., to be closer to you).

10. If there is a waiting period before benefits are payable, make sure your parents can afford to pay costs until the policy starts paying benefits.

11. See if the policy covers skilled nursing care, intermediate care, custodial care, and home health care.

12. See if the policy covers adult day-care to allow your parents to live at home longer. Home day-care can provide a psychological benefit for your parents by allowing them to live at home and reduce the drain on their assets. Day-care costs are usually much less expensive than nursing home costs.

Make sure the insurance company is financially sound with a high rating from insurance ratings services such as A.M. Best, Moody's and Standard & Poor's. Each of these services describes their rating system as to what constitutes a high or low ranking.

Government assistance in paying for nursing home costs

Your parent(s) may qualify for long-term care at government expense and still keep assets and income in the family. You and your parents will need legal advice as far in advance as possible because there are timing requirements that must be followed for certain steps.

Among the questions to be discussed with an attorney are:

1. Which assets can be preserved for a spouse and/or other members of the family and how can this be done?

2. Are gifts or transfers permissible and/or advisable and what is the appropriate timing of such actions?

3. Which assets will be subject to governmental liens or claims and when would the state go after such assets?

4. How should beneficiary designations, wills, trusts, and possibly powers of attorney be coordinated with this planning?

5. What are the effects of parents moving to another state?

It may not be too late to take steps

You may feel it's too late for your parent or parents to take action to preserve assets for the family. Even if one of your parents is in a nursing home, certain steps may still be available. Your parents can consult an attorney to see what options are available to preserve assets and income for the family and still qualify for government assistance in paying nursing home costs.

This is an area where the law keeps changing so it is important to have up-to-date information from an attorney who stays current on these matters. A possible source for an attorney is the National Academy of Elder Law Attorneys (1604 N. Country Club Road, Tucson AZ 85716, 602/881-4005).

42.

New nursing home insurance program may give special protection to your parents' assets

In 1993 Congress passed a law requiring states to attempt to recover nursing home costs from estates of deceased persons (including the estate of a surviving spouse) where those costs were paid by the government.

A new kind of long-term care insurance policy (through assistance from the Robert Wood Johnson Foundation) could protect your parents' assets from the cost recovery program. This new insurance is only available in a few states (California, Connecticut, Indiana, and New York).

What is unique about this insurance is that it may allow someone to qualify for governmental aid and be exempt from state recovery efforts. That's because the policy does two things at once: (1) it reimburses the government for benefits given to your parents, and (2) it may exempt an equivalent amount of your parents' assets from these recovery efforts.

Thus, a person having some or even considerable assets could qualify for government assistance with nursing home costs and still protect one's assets.

This exemption will probably be available only up to the amount of this new long-term care insurance that's actually purchased. Some states may be more liberal and exempt an unlimited amount of assets as long as a minimum size policy is purchased.

This insurance policy may protect assets, but not income, after the insurance benefits are exhausted. Also, not all of the costs of living and care will be paid by this type of insurance.

Your parents will need to review the insurance plans and eligibility requirements with their attorney.

This new insurance will not be available to everyone. Among the factors that may make one ineligible are pre-existing conditions and one's state of residency. And, not everyone will be able to afford this insurance.

As with any new law, it may take a long time to work out the details.

LOOKING OUT
FOR YOUR PARENTS

43.

Telling your parents the financial facts of life before they remarry

In Nos. 24 through 30 on pages 77 through 88, you read about the many issues you face when you marry or remarry. These same issues apply to your parents, too, and there may even be another issue.

When our parents marry a new spouse, they very often want their assets to go to their children and family.

Assuming the new couple (1) signs a marital agreement saying what's mine is mine and what's yours is yours, (2) signs new wills and/or trusts, (3) coordinates how title (ownership) on assets is set up so that it works with and not against the wills and trusts, and (4) signs any needed waivers on retirement plan benefits to allow children to benefit, there is still another issue for your parents to consider.

What will happen to the assets of *both* spouses if shortly after the remarriage, the senior citizen bride or groom needs long-term nursing home care? The expectation of the couple might be that the assets of the well spouse cannot be touched. Most people would imagine that once the assets of the ill spouse were exhausted, then governmental aid for nursing home costs could be obtained.

However, the law in your parent's state may delay governmental assistance until some or most of the assets of the well spouse are used to pay for nursing home costs (or the government might be able to make a claim against the assets of the well spouse after the death of the well spouse). Legal advice should be obtained to see how the law works in your parent's state.

This scenario may mean that this short remarriage results in depriving one of the ability to pass on an inheritance from a lifetime of work to one's children. Even worse, this is a case where saying "I do" can really mean saying "I'm elderly and could soon be broke."

Take a look at the strategies discussed in No. 41 and No. 42 on pages 111 through 116 to help protect your parent from this situation.

44.

Helping your parents after you're gone

You may feel that your parents will always have enough to live on.

Since we can never know for sure, you may want to plan for them in your will or living trust with a *rainy day trust* that only comes into play after you pass away. A rainy day trust says that a portion of your assets could only be used after your parents' assets were exhausted or unavailable.

However, ask your attorney how a rainy day trust might affect government assistance for the payment of nursing home costs for your parents.

45.

Avoiding liability for your parents' medical costs

Chances are your parents may need to go to a hospital or nursing home at some point. You may be asked to "just sign a few forms" to get them admitted. Be careful because you may be signing a bigger commitment than you have in mind.

When you sign such forms, are you signing a blank check by agreeing to be financially responsible for all charges and bills?

There are federal laws to help protect against liability in such situations but these laws may not help you, especially if your parent later transfers assets away to other siblings or relatives.

Before the situation arises, call your attorney for a relaxed explanation of the proper procedure for you to follow. Call your attorney again when this potential situation actually arises to make sure the same advice still applies.

46.

Making sure your parents' health coverage doesn't expire at the border

Before your parents plan their next vacation, make sure their health coverage doesn't run out at the border.

Medicare provides limited coverage for medical services provided outside of the U.S. Make sure that any medical expenses incurred by your parents during a cruise or trip outside the U.S. are covered under a supplemental health insurance policy or under a travel insurance policy.

47.

Medical decisions away from home

If your parents split their time between two states, they should plan for health decisions that might arise in either state since laws vary from state to state.

In general, a health directive signed according to the laws of one state may only be valid in that state. So, your parents will probably need to see an attorney in each state to have health directives signed for both states. For more information on health documents, see No. 52 on pages 132 and 133 and No. 65 on pages 170 and 171.

48.

The joint tenancy surprise: the down side of holding title as joint tenants

Joint tenancy (see also pages 77 and 95) means more than just a way to avoid probate in the event of a death. It can also have negative effects when parents and children hold ownership to assets together as joint tenants.

Financial risk of joint tenancy

If your parents put you and/or your brothers and sisters (or anyone else) on title as joint tenants on any of their assets, all of the joint tenants are co-owners of the assets (e.g., a house) while your parents are alive.

Besides gift tax, income tax, property tax, and death tax issues arising from joint tenancy, parents are taking a financial risk when they hold title as joint tenants with their children.

Although joint tenancy may afford more protection from creditors after the death of one of the joint tenants (see No. 35 on page 95), it can lead to more exposure to creditors while all the joint tenants are alive.

If, for example, one of your brothers or sisters has a business that goes under, then the creditors of that sibling may go after the sibling's portion of your parents' house while your parents are alive. If one of your siblings is at fault in a car accident where their car insurance is not enough to cover the damage, the injured party may also go after your sibling's portion of your parents' house while your parents are alive. In either of these examples the creditor could become a co-owner with your parents or possibly force a sale of the house (maybe even charge your parents rent for the interest in the house owned by the creditor).

So, if your parents want to avoid probate and also avoid being responsible for their children's debts and actions, they should talk to their attorney about setting up a *living trust* instead. A living trust is an arrangement that spells out who is to be the manager and beneficiary of assets while your parents are alive and after each of them passes away. A living trust, which is in essence a substitute for a will, allows successors to avoid the probate court after a death. (To be fully effective, however, certain asset transfers need to be done before a death.)

The bottom line is that while a technique such as joint tenancy may be good for one purpose (e.g., avoiding probate), it can have other, unintended, disastrous effects.

Also, if parents and children hold title as joint tenants and pass away simultaneously, such as in a car accident or a plane crash, the jointly held assets (e.g., a house, bank accounts, stocks, etc.) may go through several probates: the parents' and the children's. So, in such cases joint tenancy may not even give the benefit of avoiding probate.

Joint tenancy may disinherit intended beneficiaries

What do you think happens in this scenario: Your parents sign wills leaving everything equally to all of their four children, including you. They put one of your siblings on title to everything they own as a joint tenant. Both of your parents pass away. Who gets your parents' assets?

In general, it's going to be one person, the one sibling who was on title as a joint tenant.

126

A will or trust generally does not control assets held in joint tenancy. Unless an exception applies, assets held in joint tenancy pass outside of a will or trust to the surviving joint tenant.

In the above example, your parents probably wanted the one child to be able sign checks or take actions on their behalf if they became disabled. They probably did not want to give all of their assets to the one child.

Again, a living trust might be a safer way of dealing with disability or incompetency.

The bottom line is that you and your siblings should not have to face the joint tenancy surprise. Encourage your parents to see an attorney who can explain their options to them.

49.

How to postpone or reduce property taxes

Your parents may own a home and need extra cash. They may be able to have that extra cash by postponing the payment of property taxes. Some states allow such a postponement which is really a low-interest loan. The taxes and interest usually need to be paid back when the house is sold or your parents pass away.

Besides postponing property taxes, there may be ways to reduce or at least avoid increases in property taxes, too.

Your parents' house may have been overvalued by the tax assessor. It may be easy and worthwhile to question the assessment.

For those over a certain age (e.g., age 55), some states allow property taxes to stay the same after selling a house and buying another in the same state.

There may also be a way for parents or step-parents to reduce the property tax on real estate they give or leave in a will or trust to their children (and step-children). Certain states allow property taxes to stay at the same level when children inherit or receive the real estate as a gift even if the property is worth far more than the original purchase price paid for by the parents (or step-parents).

This benefit may not apply for portions received or inherited by *grandchildren*. So, if your parents were thinking of dividing up real estate and other assets to children and grandchildren, it might make financial sense to allocate the real estate more, or only, to the children and other assets to the grandchildren. The difference in property tax payments can be significant, especially if the property is retained for many years.

50.

The income tax surprise all siblings need to know

If your parents leave you and your sibling equal shares of their estate, you can accidentally wind up with less than your sibling. Your share may be the one that's subject to income tax.

Assume that your parents have two main assets (their house and their IRAs) and they are thinking of leaving them to their two children—you and your sibling.

If the house is worth about the same as the IRAs and you and your sibling don't get along well, your parents might think they were doing you a favor (and not harming either of you in any way) by leaving the house to your sibling and the IRAs to you. After all, this would avoid co-ownership and possibly fights between you and your sibling.

Your parents unfortunately made this decision before obtaining legal and tax advice so they weren't aware of the different consequences to you and your sibling. If your sibling inherits the house, it won't be income to him or her in the eyes of Uncle Sam (unless and until the house is sold for a profit). If you receive the IRAs, it *will* be income to you and you'll be paying income tax on all or a portion of the amounts received. The solution is for your parents to get legal advice so their estates are planned properly.

51.

The death tax surprise
all siblings need to know

Depending on how your parents' wills, trusts and beneficiary designations read, you may have the pleasure of paying death tax on assets inherited by your sibling.

Very often, wills and trusts stipulate that all the death taxes be paid from the "residue" of the estate covered by the documents.

Certain assets may pass automatically outside a will or trust upon a death such as joint tenancy assets and assets that have beneficiary designations (e.g., IRAs and life insurance).

Assume that your parents have two main assets (their house and their IRAs) and death tax will be due. In their wills they leave the house to you and they leave the IRAs under beneficiary designations to your sibling.

The wills might say death taxes on everything (including assets passing outside the will such as IRAs) will be paid from the assets (the house) covered by the will. This means that you would pay the death taxes on the house you inherited and on the IRAs *inherited by your sibling*. Is this what your parents intended? Again, make sure your parents get legal advice to properly plan their estates to avoid this tax result.

52.

Mentioning the unmentionable

We all have a reluctance to discuss terminal illness and death. Your parents should discuss both of these issues with the family and put their desires in writing. You should do the same to help your loved ones.

Terminal illness

There are two basic legal documents for handling a terminal illness: (1) a *health power of attorney* and (2) a *living will* (also sometimes called a *directive to physician* or *natural death declaration*). (See also pages 170 and 171 for further discussion.)

A health power of attorney appoints an agent to make all the big and small health care decisions if one isn't able to speak for himself or herself. The biggest decision is whether to "pull the plug" (i.e., to be taken off life-support machines).

Your parents need to completely trust the agent they are naming. They should consider whether that person has any financial conflict of interest. For example, will the agent inherit from your parents if the plug is pulled? Often that's the case but that fact alone shouldn't rule a person out. Also, the agent should not have personal or religious beliefs that would prevent fulfillment of your parents' desired wishes.

The *living will* deals just with the big issue, pulling the plug. It's usually put into effect if there's an incurable and irreversible condition that has been diagnosed by two physicians and the condition either (1) will result in death within a relatively short time without the administration of life-sustaining treatment, or (2) has produced an irreversible coma or persistent vegetative state in which one is no longer able to make decisions regarding his or her medical treatment. Under such circumstances, a living will directs the attending physician to withhold or withdraw treatment that only prolongs an irreversible coma, a persistent vegetative state, or the process of dying. Such treatment is defined as "not necessary for your comfort or to alleviate pain" and could include the use of a respirator as well as artificially administered nutrition and hydration.

Spelling out funeral arrangements

If a will spells out funeral arrangements and is placed in a safe deposit box, it's possible no one may have access to the box until after the funeral is over.

Loved ones (and one's executor) should know in advance what is desired and also whether any arrangements have been made such as prepaid funeral or cremation costs.

Expressing desires in writing can avoid confusion or misunderstandings at a time when everyone is grieving.

A direction for funeral arrangements should cover at least the following items:

1. The nature of the desired ceremony (if any)—indicate whether it's to be religious or non-religious, elaborate or private
2. Name, address, phone number and title of person to officiate and any special readings, passages or prayers to be included as part of the service
3. Location of ceremony
4. Name and location of cemetery
5. Burial or cremation
6. Any prepayments that have been made

7. If a burial, location of plot/crypt
8. If cremation, disposition of ashes
9. Headstone/monument requests
10. Donation of body organs.

INSURING YOUR RETIREMENT

53.

The three questions you should ask about life insurance—before you buy

Before you buy life insurance, always ask yourself *and* your life insurance agent these three questions:

1. Why do I need this insurance?

2. What is the most this policy will cost me and for how many years under a worst-case scenario?

3. How much will I lose if I decide to cancel the policy early?

Do you need life insurance?

The first step in deciding whether to purchase life insurance is to determine your needs, which could include any of the following:

1. Making life more comfortable for a surviving spouse and/or children

2. Having enough money to raise and educate children in case of a death

3. Having a ready source of cash to pay death taxes so assets such as real estate or a family business don't have to be liquidated to meet tax obligations

4. Providing the funds to buy out the interest of a business partner if the partner dies

5. Paying for funeral costs and legal expenses upon a death

6. Building up a source of retirement income and assets.

If you have more than one need, then you may want more than one policy and/or more than one type of policy (for types of policies, see No. 54 on pages 139 to 145).

Not everyone, however, needs life insurance. For example, single persons with no dependents (i.e., no children or parents or other individuals dependent on them) may not need any life insurance other than to cover funeral costs.

Worst-case scenario

Before you purchase life insurance, you are usually handed a lengthy computer printout. On the printout are many columns with calculations explaining the cost and benefits of a policy.

This printout includes an optimistic projection (estimate) of your future costs and benefits. This is a non-guaranteed estimate. You need to see in writing what the guaranteed result would be. In other words, what is the worst-case scenario as far as:

1. The number of years you will have to pay premiums

2. The amount of those premiums and how they might increase over the years

3. How low the benefits could drop.

Cost of dropping a policy early

Some insurance policies build up a "cash value" for you. You should find out what would be left of that cash value if you dropped a policy after 1, 5, 10, or 20 years.

54.

Buying the right amount and kind of life insurance

To determine the right amount and kind of life insurance you need, first analyze your purpose in buying the policy (see also No. 54 on pages 137 and 138).

For example, if the policy is to help pay for death taxes (see also No. 23 on pages 71 to 74 and No. 55 on page 146), you need to decide whether you are going to insure for the current value of your estate, a projected future value dependent upon your life expectancy and inflation rates, or something in between.

For a policy that is taken out to help support a spouse and/or children, you should go through the following four steps with your life insurance agent, financial advisor, and/or attorney to determine the right amount of life insurance.

Step One: Calculate your net worth

This involves looking at what you have and what you owe. Be realistic in adding up your assets and subtracting your liabilities (the result is your *net worth*).

Savings accounts, life insurance, retirement plans, and stocks are assets that can provide ready cash for your estate. If you are married, calculate what will be available, including life insurance, in the event of (1) your death, (2) your spouse's death, and (3) both of your deaths. For other assets such as real estate (that your children won't be living in), estimate the sales price of your assets after you're gone.

As for your liabilities, identify when large payments on debts will be due. In particular, are there regular mortgage payments on your house or investment property that are spread out evenly over 15 or 30 years or is there a balloon (i.e., large) payment that's due next year or in five years?

Step Two: Add up death-related costs and expenses

To do this, subtract from your net worth the expected death tax, income tax, attorney's fees, executor's (or trustee's) fees, and other death-related costs (such as funeral expenses).

Step Three: Determine the future needs of your children and/or spouse

This entails looking at your children's (and possibly your spouse's) circumstances. How much you want to have on hand for small children can be a very different story compared to grown children who are financially comfortable on their own (a rarity these days, to be sure). Also, you may have one or more young or adult children who have special disabilities that require additional resources.

What standard of living do you want your spouse or children to have? Do you want your children to be able to attend private school as a youngster as well as a private college as an adult? What about money for their graduate studies, too?

Where will your young children be living if you're not around? Will the people you're naming as their guardian need to add on to their house to have your children live there, too? Are you able to provide for that?

Step Four: Putting it all together to determine your insurance requirements

This step requires that you take all of the information from the first three steps and work backwards to come up with the necessary amount to leave for your children and/or spouse.

Begin by estimating the future income from your assets. Since we don't know what the future holds in the economy, you'll probably want to see results from different growth (e.g., 4%, 6%, 8%, and 10%) and inflation rates (e.g., 4%, 6%, and 8%).

Next, you should estimate how much your spouse and children will need per year (such as $10,000 for one child and $15,000 for another child) and build an inflation factor in these expenses, too. Consider how much your family will be receiving from Social Security for survivors benefits.

Once you calculate the expected income and expenses over the years, you'll be able to see how long your money will last. Will your money be gone before all of your children are age 21? Age 18? Age 12?

The last question is whether you want some money left over to give to your children after they attain a certain age (for example, age 21).

Use these four steps and make any necessary adjustments to calculate the sum of money you'll need to have on hand to provide for your family. A rule of thumb is to insure for five to eight times your annual salary in taking care of young children. If you have many children and just two thumbs, this rule may be too expensive to follow.

Do you want the IRS as a beneficiary on your life insurance?

You should remember that some of the insurance proceeds may go to the IRS instead of to your family, depending upon the size of your estate and the way you own life insurance. Talk to your attorney (and see No. 55 on page 146) about ways to insure that life insurance passes to your family free of federal death tax.

Types of policies and uses

Once you decide how much life insurance you need, the next step is to decide on the right kind of insurance for you.

There are two main types of life insurance: *cash value* and *term*. There are variations of each type of policy and some policies combine both types of insurance within one policy package.

Term insurance

Term insurance is the easier one to understand. Term insurance is like renting insurance—as long as you pay your premium, a death benefit will be paid. You don't own anything with term insurance. If you stop paying the premium, you walk away with nothing and no death benefit is payable.

Term insurance is more appropriate for shorter-term needs. For example, if you have children who are college-age or younger, you might want to be sure that there is enough money to educate them or to provide for them to age 18 or 21.

One mistake that is often made in families where both spouses work is the assumption that the kids will be able to get by, if they have to, on the income of one spouse. Well, what happens to that theory if both spouses pass away in a car accident? It's no fun thinking about the terrible possibilities that are out there, but part of the responsibility of being a parent is to make sure children are provided for in any eventuality. So, consider insuring each spouse.

Term insurance premium costs are initially lower than cash value life insurance but they may increase rapidly as one gets older (since the risk of dying increases over time, too).

You can have term insurance and at the same time keep premiums at the same level rate by purchasing *level premium term insurance*. With this type of insurance, the premium stays at the same cost for a specified period of time, such as 7 years, 10 years, or 15 years.

Since cost is a factor, always determine the cost of term insurance (including level term insurance) before making your decision.

If you are getting term insurance, purchase an annual renewable term policy so you don't have to pass physical exams each year to keep the policy as long as you want it.

Cash value life insurance

Cash value life insurance is a combination of term insurance (it provides a death benefit) with a tax-deferred investment component.

Cash value life insurance is generally intended to be lifelong insurance (rather than for a shorter term) and it costs more than term insurance in the earlier years.

There are many variations of cash value life insurance. They range from conservative to more risky in their operation and effect. In general, all types of cash value life policies allow for tax-deferred growth and non-taxable distributions through loans and withdrawals.

The most conservative type is *traditional whole life insurance.* There are more guarantees on the ultimate premiums and benefits with this type of cash value life insurance. One use is as a source to pay death taxes.

A variation on traditional whole life insurance that has greater risk (and possibly greater rewards or losses) is *universal* (or *flexible* or *adjustable*) *life insurance.* With this type of insurance, a policyholder gets some flexibility in the amount of premium that needs to be paid each year and the amount of life insurance in place at any given time. Younger people with changing needs and the willingness to take risks often look to this type of policy.

Another variation is called *variable insurance.* It is similar to traditional whole life or universal life insurance but the investment component is very often put in mutual funds. It's the riskiest because if the investments do not work out, you can lose not only your cash value in the policy *but also* your coverage as well. However, if the investments do work out, you can reduce the size of your premium payments.

The potential candidates for this type of insurance are usually persons who need life insurance and have fully utilized the other tax-deferral vehicles such as retirement plans (including IRAs, 401(k) plans, and Keogh plans). Again, younger people with changing needs and the willingness to take risks often look to this type of policy.

Special life insurance for married couples

Spouses can also purchase permanent insurance that pays either (1) on the first death or (2) on the second death of two insureds.

The first type of policy, often called *first-to-die insurance,* can be used for a family where both spouses work and the survivor would need insurance to replace the income of the spouse who died.

The second type of policy, often called *second-to-die insurance,* is commonly used to replenish an estate for death taxes that will be due on the death of the second spouse. This type of policy is generally less expensive than two separate policies because it is covering the lives of two people but the insurance company is paying off only one time, and only after two insureds have passed away.

Get a sound company

As with any insurance, make sure the insurance company is rated highly by A.M. Best, Moody's, Standard & Poor's, Weiss Research and Duff & Phelps.

You could reduce your risk on any sizeable amount of insurance by using two companies rather than one. You'll need to compare any extra cost with the comfort you'll receive splitting the coverage between two companies.

Since life insurance is a long-term investment, you'll need a well established and financially sound company when the time comes to collect proceeds.

55.

Secret ways to avoid death tax on life insurance

In general, each person can bequeath up to $600,000 (the *federal death tax exemption* limit) with no federal death tax (spouses can leave an unlimited amount to each other with no death tax until both spouses are gone).

Most people think you don't count life insurance when you are determining that $600,000 figure. Actually, it depends.

If life insurance pushes you over the $600,000 federal death tax exemption limit (or if you're already above that amount), your estate could land in the taxing zone, a zone that starts at the 37% rate and goes up from there.

What this means is that a good portion or even a majority of the insurance policy proceeds on your death could go to *Uncle Sam* rather than to your family. If you don't do advance planning, you might as well name Uncle Sam on the beneficiary designation form.

There are two ways, however, to keep the insurance proceeds from being taxable for death tax purposes: either have an *irrevocable life insurance trust* (i.e., a trust that cannot be changed) or have your children own, apply for, and pay for the policy.

Ask your attorney whether a life insurance trust or direct ownership (and premium payments) by your children makes sense for you. The time to ask about all of this is before you apply for a policy although certain steps can be taken to utilize existing policies, too.

56.

The right and wrong way to name beneficiaries

Beneficiary designations generally override your will or trust.

If the beneficiaries under your will or trust differ from those selected in other designations (e.g., life insurance, retirement plan, and IRA), you should make it clear in your will or trust that this has been done intentionally. This will avoid potentially costly fights and help keep family harmony. Also, consider the income tax and death tax ramifications resulting from beneficiary designations (see No. 50 and No. 51 on pages 130 and 131).

Three overlooked issues in beneficiary designations

The first issue involves the consequences of failing to specify a secondary or contingent beneficiary on a beneficiary form. If your primary beneficiary does not survive you, that can mean in many cases that the benefits will be paid to your estate.

There are two main problems with benefits going into your estate. First, the benefits become subject to attorney's and executor's fees and delays that might otherwise have been avoided. Second, if the benefits are paid to your estate, an asset that may have been exempt from creditors' claims might well be converted to one that could be taken by creditors.

The second overlooked issue in beneficiary designations involves failing to specify what will happen to the benefits earmarked for a child if the child does not outlive you but leaves a child (your grandchild) who does survive you. Your beneficiary designation can be worded to deal with this possibility.

The third issue concerns whether you've named individual(s) or a trust on your beneficiary designation. Who you name as beneficiaries can determine how long income tax may be postponed on certain retirement benefits. Your attorney and tax advisor can tell whether this tax postponement possibility is available to you.

Keep designations current

Always keep your beneficiary designations up to date to reflect your current intent and do so with the assistance of legal advice to make sure the designation works with, and not against, your estate plan.

57.

Receiving disability insurance benefits income-tax free

If you become disabled and receive benefits under a disability insurance policy, those benefits may or may not be free of income tax. Since income tax rates are climbing higher, this could be extremely important to you while you are disabled.

In general, if you personally pay the insurance premiums as compared to a company paying the premiums, the benefits will be income-tax free to you. If, instead, your employer pays the premiums, then the benefits will be subject to income tax. Be sure to review this topic with your disability insurance agent, accountant, and attorney.

58.

What to look for in a disability insurance policy

Disability policies are not all the same. They can vary widely in cost and benefits. In general, there are two benefits from purchasing a policy while you are younger: (1) the cost is lower and (2) you are still insurable and not subject to a health condition that may disqualify you from coverage.

When you find a policy, see how it handles at least the following seven items:

1. Check if the benefits are payable for life (or at least until age 65) instead of a maximum period such as for five years.

2. See if the benefits (a) increase with inflation (i.e., is there a "cost-of-living adjustment" or "COLA"?) or (b) give you options to increase coverage over time without the requirement of a physical examination rather than just staying a fixed dollar amount during the life of the policy.

3. Review the definition of the term *disability* in the policy to see if benefits will be paid if you can't work in your *current occupation* or only if you can't do *any kind of work*.

4. Calculate how long you can afford to wait before the benefits become payable—one month, three months, one year. The longer the waiting period, the lower the premium. Don't be overly optimistic about your ability

to survive financially while you are disabled. A three-month waiting period might be realistic for you.

5. Since partial disabilities are not uncommon, check to see if partial disability benefits are included without having to be totally disabled.

6. See whether premiums are waived (excused) if you are disabled.

7. Read the policy to be sure you understand the exclusions under the policy.

TAKING CARE
OF BUSINESS

59.

Getting down to business: incorporation

If you own or co-own a business, including a home-based business, don't overlook the protection afforded by incorporating the business.

If that great idea for a business doesn't pan out, you may be able to save your personal assets owned outside the corporation if all proper steps have been taken in the formation and operation of the corporation.

You may receive special income tax benefits through tax elections such as an *S Corporation election.*

Ask your attorney and accountant about the benefits and costs of incorporating your business. And, ask your liability insurance agent about obtaining sufficient coverage against the mishaps of daily business life.

60.

Three steps every business owner has to consider

Nearly 90% of U.S. businesses are family businesses. You may be a part or sole owner of such a business. Since fewer than one in three family businesses survives into the second generation, you may need to deal with a few family business facts of life.

Every business owner needs to consider taking the following three steps:

1. Sign a written agreement dealing with future ownership of the business.

   Are you involved in a family business with one or both of your parents? Your siblings? Your children? You probably need a written agreement covering the succession of ownership in the event of death or disability.

   Will one or more of your children want to sell their shares to outsiders without giving the other children a chance to match any outside offer? Will you want to restrict their ability to do so with a written agreement?

2. Have a will or trust that considers family involvement or non-involvement of children in the business.

   Are only some of your children working in the family business? If you passed away, you might want *only* the children working in the business to inherit it from you.

If you left the business to all the children, it might create problems for them. The "non-working children" might want larger non-deductible dividends paid to them rather than the reinvestment of profits into the business. The working children might try to have the business pay them exorbitant salaries to reduce the profits paid out to the non-working children.

If possible, you might want to leave the business only to the children working in the business. The other children would then receive other assets. If you don't have other assets comparable in value to the business, you might want to use life insurance to equalize the amount of assets passing to all of your children.

3. Plan in advance the sources to pay death taxes.

Death taxes may force the business to be sold no matter what agreement has been signed. Instead, life insurance could provide the funds to pay death taxes so the operation of the business could continue unaffected. See No. 55 on page 146 for ways to avoid death tax on the life insurance proceeds.

An agreement for succession of ownership of the business as well as coordinated wills, trusts, and life insurance policies can produce a smooth and equitable result for all of your family.

61.

What you need to know if you have a partner in real estate or business

If you have a partner in real estate or business, you need to prepare yourself for what the future may hold for your partnership with respect to your estate planning.

Depending upon how you hold title (ownership) with your partner, the partner may receive those assets upon your death.

That's because you may hold title in a way that overrides your will or trust so that your share automatically passes to your partner. You should have your attorney check title to your assets so that your intended beneficiaries receive your assets upon your death.

To add insult to injury, it's possible that unless you take steps to prevent it, your loved ones would have to pay death taxes on assets going to your partner.

You might also want to have a written agreement with your partner giving you an option to buy out your partner's interest in the business or real estate if your partner dies, becomes disabled, or just wants to sell his or her interest. Otherwise, you might end up co-owning the real estate or business with strangers or your partner's children.

MAKING MONEY FROM YOUR PAPERWORK

62.

How financial records can save you taxes on your house

Having organized financial records can save you income taxes when you sell your house.

Selling your house

You may owe income tax when you sell your house. Although there are ways to postpone paying income tax if you purchase another house, at some point you may have to pay the piper. (See No. 14 on pages 40 and 41 on how the gain may not be taxed at all.)

When you sell your house, income tax may be due on the gain above your original cost plus improvements. You need to have organized records to keep track of the improvements that may reduce the income tax due on a sale. You should set up a separate file that makes it easy to store and locate the invoices and checks to substantiate the improvements made to your house.

And, if there still is taxable gain after reducing your profit by the improvements, take a look at No. 26 on pages 80 to 82 for a possible way to exclude another $125,000 in gain.

63.

How financial records can save you taxes on stocks and mutual funds

If you invest in stocks or mutual funds, from time to time you'll want or need to sell shares to buy a house, pay for your children's college education, or take a needed vacation.

Stocks or mutual funds may be in a tax-deferred investment (e.g., IRA) that will grow income-tax free until distributions are taken out.

However, you may own such stocks or funds just in your own name and sales would be subject to income tax. You may be able to reduce or eliminate the income tax on such a sale of stock or mutual fund share if you have organized records.

If an investment has gone up in value since you purchased it, you will owe income tax on the sale of that investment. Very often you will purchase additional shares over time. Will you owe income tax if some of the investment has gone up and some has gone down in value since you purchased it?

With organized records, you could direct the sale of those portions of your stock or mutual fund shares that produced the lowest income tax due. Check with your accountant as to the various tax methods available for determining gain or loss on the sale of stocks and mutual funds.

How to avoid paying extra, unnecessary income tax

If you invest in a mutual fund and reinvest the dividends rather than take them out, organized records may allow you to reduce the gain upon a sale.

Suppose you put $1,000 into a fund and over the years you receive $300 in dividends, which are reinvested in the fund. You now have $1,300 invested. When you decide to sell your interest in the fund for $2,000, good records will show that you have $700 of gain ($2,000 less $1,300) not $1,000 of gain ($2,000 less $1,000) since the reinvested dividends were previously taxed.

DEALING WITH INCAPACITY

64.

Who do you trust—with your money?

When you are incapacitated, more than ever you need someone you can trust to handle your money and other assets. If you don't take steps before an incapacity to name your choice or choices, you're taking quite a chance as to who will be in charge of your assets.

If you want to name your choices in advance, you can do so in three main documents: a *nomination of conservator*, a *living trust*, or a *power of attorney*.

If you become incapacitated, a court may become involved in the management of your assets through a proceeding known generally as a *conservatorship* (sometimes called a *guardianship*). Whether a court-appointed *conservator* (i.e, a person or bank who becomes the manager of your assets) is required depends upon how title (ownership) reads on your assets and whether you have signed a living trust or power of attorney.

With some documents (a *living trust* or *power of attorney*), court may be avoided. Your agent, under these documents, is put in charge fairly informally and there is no court supervision as to what is done with your money and other assets. These documents may save a considerable amount in attorney's fees and court costs.

The potential disadvantage with these documents is that there is not a court system looking over the shoulder of the person handling your assets. This may not be a problem if you appoint trustworthy people to handle your assets while you are incapacitated.

One way of hedging your bets is to name two people acting together instead of just one person.

As we and our parents age, more thought must be given to how assets will be managed in the event of incapacity.

Depending upon state law and personal preferences, a power of attorney could include the following powers to:

1. Create, amend or revoke a living trust or create an irrevocable trust
2. Place assets in a trust
3. Deal with the Internal Revenue Service
4. Make gifts to save death taxes or take steps to keep assets in the family
5. Change beneficiaries on life insurance and retirement plans
6. Handle retirement plan distributions
7. Push away or disclaim inheritances, gifts, life insurance or retirement benefits for tax reasons
8. Change the person's permanent personal residence (*domicile*)—this can have significant implications for eligibility for governmental assistance for nursing home costs.

Remember, if you sign a power of attorney, you may be signing the equivalent of a blank check with the powers you are giving your agent.

Conflict of interest

Whenever you name someone in a document to act on your behalf, always think about whether that agent would have a conflict of interest and might act for the agent's best interests and not yours. If you name someone to manage and be in charge of spending your assets and that person is also the beneficiary under your will or trust, might the agent hold back on medical or other expenditures on your behalf with the hope of inheriting more and/or sooner? If so, you need to name someone else to act on your behalf.

65.

Who do you trust—with your life?

What can you do to avoid the prolonging of life if you have a terminal illness and the pain and lack of quality outweigh the benefits? What if you are concerned that medical bills in a futile situation will eat up all your assets?

You need to express your desires before you're unable to speak for yourself. The best way is to have a written document that spells out what you want done and what you don't want done in a terminal illness situation.

There are two basic documents for you to explore: (1) a *health power of attorney* and (2) a *living will* (also sometimes called a *directive to physician* or *natural death declaration*).

A health power of attorney appoints an agent to decide big and small health care decisions if you cannot speak for yourself. The biggest decision, of course, is whether to "pull the plug" (i.e., to be taken off life-support machines). A lesser decision might be to choose between two possible operations (when you're unconscious at the time but not in a life-threatening situation).

You need to have complete trust in the agent you are naming. You should consider whether that person has any financial conflict of interest. For example, will that person inherit from you if the plug is pulled for you? Since the people you select as your agent usually inherit from you too, you should not rule out those persons just because of their status as a beneficiary. However, keep this possible conflict in mind. Also, be sure that the persons you select do not have personal or religious beliefs that will prevent them from carrying out your wishes.

The living will deals just with the big issue, pulling the plug if an incurable and irreversible condition has been diagnosed by physicians and other criteria are met.

You should consider having both a health power of attorney and a living will. You may be able to take discretion away from your agent under the health power of attorney so that if the criteria of the living will are met, the plug must be pulled.

If you travel frequently to another state or have residences in more than one state, you should ask your attorney about signing forms in more than one state since states usually have their own forms. At this time, there is no form that is automatically binding in every state—however, having a copy of signed forms in your possession could very likely result in your wishes being honored out of state, too.

Appendix

Examples of Social Security Retirement, Disability and Survivors benefits

Retirement benefit examples

For these examples* of monthly Social Security retirement benefits, assume you and your spouse are age 45 in 1994, you have had steady lifetime earnings and retire at full retirement age rather than taking an early retirement:

Your 1993 earnings	Your monthly benefit	Monthly benefit for you and your spouse
$20,000	$ 777	$1,165
30,000	1,044	1,566
40,000	1,177	1,765
50,000	1,301	1,953
57,600 or more	1,400	2,100

*Note: The accuracy of these estimates depends on the pattern of your actual past earnings and on your earnings in the future. Your actual benefit at the time of retirement in the future will be higher because these estimates are shown in today's dollars. A spouse may qualify for a higher retirement benefit based on his or her own work record.

For these examples** of monthly Social Security disability benefits, assume you are age 45 in 1994, become disabled in 1994 and had steady lifetime earnings (the following survivors benefit examples assume you passed away in 1994):

Disability benefit examples

Your 1993 earnings	Your monthly benefit	Monthly benefit for you, your spouse, and child
$20,000	$ 777	$1,166
30,000	1,044	1,567
40,000	1,177	1,759
50,000	1,266	1,899
57,600 or more	1,303	1,954

Survivors benefit examples

Your 1993 earnings	Monthly benefit for your spouse and one child	Monthly benefit for your spouse and two children
$20,000	$1,166	$1,458
30,000	1,566	1,829
40,000	1,760	2,055
50,000	1,908	2,228
57,600 or more	1,968	2,296

**Note: The accuracy of these estimates depends on the pattern of your actual past earnings and on your earnings in the future. The actual benefit will be higher because these estimates are shown in today's dollars.

Software to Do Retirement Planning Calculations: The Vanguard Retirement Planner (Version 2.0)

The Vanguard Retirement Planner (Version 2.0) is a wonderful program and a bargain to boot. It's inexpensive ($15 plus $2.50 shipping and handling), simple to install on your computer, and simple to use.

You can easily change assumptions for salary or earnings, savings, desired retirement income, inflation, rates of return, retirement age, and life expectancy, and you can see the results on screen in color graphs. The program is offered by a mutual fund company, the Vanguard Group of Investment Companies.

This program requires an IBM-compatible personal computer with a VGA, XGA, or Super VGA monitor; at least 512 kilobytes (512K) of RAM; 1.2 megabytes (1.2 MB) of free memory; and DOS version 3.0 or higher (it will run under Windows™ but it is not compatible with OS/2™). You can use a mouse or keyboard with the program. It is not for use with Apple computers. It's available on a 3½" or 5¼" high density disk.

It can be used with most printers. Call the 800 number listed below to make sure it's compatible with your computer, disk drive, and printer.

For order information call: 1/800-937-2668 (VISA or MasterCard only)

The Vanguard Retirement Planner is a registered service mark of the Vanguard Group, Inc. Microsoft Windows™ is a registered trademark of Microsoft Corporation. OS/2™ is a registered trademark of IBM Corporation.

Index

A

Accountant
    advice from, 31-32, 43, 45,
        80-82, 105, 149, 162
    financial planner
        recommended by, 15
    incorporation and, 155
    sale of residence and, 40-41,
        80-82, 161
    S Corporation election and,
        155
    Social Security and advice
        from, 56
Adjustable life insurance. *See* Life
    insurance
Alternative minimum tax, 40
Alzheimer's disease. *See also*
    Incapacity
    long-term care insurance and,
        112
Annuities, 44-49
    companies issuing, 46
    duration of, 46
    fees and early withdrawals of,
        14, 40
    financial strength of
        companies issuing, 46
    fixed-rate, 47-48
    flexible, 48
    IRAs compared to, 47-49
    mutual funds and, 49
    need for, 45-46
    nest egg compared to, 44-45
    nursing home costs and, 47
    retirement plan payouts and,
        85, 92
    single-premium, 48

Social Security and, 39
    surrender costs of, 40
    variable, 39-40, 48-49
    withdrawals from, 14, 40, 47
Ante-nuptial agreements. *See*
    Marital agreement
Assumptions
    retirement planning, 22-23, 25-
        26
    Social Security, 173-74

B

B trust. *See* Death tax
Bankruptcy
    retirement plans and, 92
Beneficiary designations
    creditors and, 92-93, 147
    death tax and, 131, 141-42,
        146, 157
    gaps and, 93, 147-48
    income tax and, 130, 148
    irrevocable life insurance trusts
        and, 97, 146, 157
    marriage and, 79, 87
    naming of beneficiaries and,
        147-48
    remarriage and, 79, 87, 148
Bonds, U.S. Savings, 60, 62
Budgets, 28-30
Business
    agreement as to, 156, 158
    creditors and, 155
    death taxes and, 157-58
    incorporation and, 155

Order Form

(Photocopy this page)

Qty.   Total

**BABY BOOMER RETIREMENT: 65 Simple Ways to
Protect Your Future by Don Silver**
208 pages $9.95 plus $1.05 s/h = **$11 per book**   ____ $_____

     Sales tax for California residents 82¢ per book $_____

**A PARENT'S GUIDE TO WILLS & TRUSTS (For
Grandparents, Too) by Don Silver**

Los Angeles Times: "Excellent book. It is clear.
It is concise. It is clever."
256 pages $11.95 plus $1.05 s/h = **$13 per book**   ____ $_____

     Sales tax for California residents 99¢ per book $_____

(FOR QUANTITY DISCOUNTS, CALL 1/800-888-4452)   Total $_____

PAYMENT PREFERENCE:
     By check, payable to Adams-Hall Publishing or
     By credit card: Visa ____   MasterCard ____
                 Discover ____   American Express ____

ACCOUNT NUMBER:_____   EXPIRATION DATE:_____

NAME ON CARD:_____
            (PLEASE PRINT CLEARLY)

     SIGNATURE:_____

PLEASE PRINT:

NAME_____

MAILING ADDRESS _____

CITY/STATE/ZIP CODE_____

DAYTIME TELEPHONE_____

**Mail to: Adams-Hall Publishing, PO Box 491002, Dept. BBR,
        Los Angeles, CA 90049 or call 1/800-888-4452 or 310/826-1851**

Order Form

(Photocopy this page)

	Qty.	Total
BABY BOOMER RETIREMENT: 65 Simple Ways to Protect Your Future by Don Silver 208 pages $9.95 plus $1.05 s/h = **$11 per book**	____	$_____
Sales tax for California residents 82¢ per book		$_____

A PARENT'S GUIDE TO WILLS & TRUSTS (For Grandparents, Too) by Don Silver

Los Angeles Times: "Excellent book. It is clear. It is concise. It is clever."

	Qty.	Total
256 pages $11.95 plus $1.05 s/h = **$13 per book**	____	$_____
Sales tax for California residents 99¢ per book		$_____

(FOR QUANTITY DISCOUNTS, CALL 1/800-888-4452) Total $_____

PAYMENT PREFERENCE:
By check, payable to Adams-Hall Publishing or
By credit card: Visa ___ MasterCard ___
Discover ___ American Express ___

ACCOUNT NUMBER:_____ EXPIRATION DATE:_____

NAME ON CARD:_____
(PLEASE PRINT CLEARLY)

SIGNATURE:_____

PLEASE PRINT:

NAME_____

MAILING ADDRESS _____

CITY/STATE/ZIP CODE_____

DAYTIME TELEPHONE_____

Mail to: Adams-Hall Publishing, PO Box 491002, Dept. BBR,
Los Angeles, CA 90049 or call 1/800-888-4452 or 310/826-1851